SELF-LOVE FOR WOMEN

11 Strategies to Cultivate Self-Worth, Embrace Yourself, Eliminate Toxic Relationships, and Teach Yourself to Love and Accept Every Aspect of Who You Are

WRITTEN BY
CAROLYN GOLFORB GODDARD

TABLE OF CONTENTS

Introduction

Chapter 1: How Do I Discover Who I Really Am?..................................8

Chapter 2: Killing Perfectionism..15

Chapter 3: Calming & Controlling the Negative Mind......................21

Chapter 4: Getting Comfortable with All of Your Emotions...............31

Chapter 5: You Deserve More Than Toxic Relationships....................37

Chapter 6: Protecting Yourself with Essential Boundaries................48

Chapter 7: Self-Care Equals Self-Love....................................55

Chapter 8: Managing Your Stress Before It Manages You.................63

Chapter 9: Completing The Package: Self-Esteem & Self-Worth........71

Chapter 10: Growing as an Empowered Woman..........................80

Chapter 11: Daily Self-Love Practices....................................85

Conclusion...94

Bonus Resources......................................96

Dedicated to Melissa, Cat, & Callie.
Three of the strongest women I've ever known.

Carolyn grew up with two incredibly influential grandmothers. They were strong women who, despite living in the more challenging and antiquated times for women, led their lives the way they wanted to and the way they deserved. They raised strong families who stuck to their convictions and were matriarchs of huge families that are still thriving today. Their legacies are alive and well.

Not only were their emotional hearts and bonds strong, but their bodies fought long and hard. Both women battled against cancer for years. Carolyn lost her paternal grandmother when she was young, and her maternal grandmother passed away when Carolyn was a teenager. Both losses hit her and her family extremely hard. Not only had they lost mothers, grandmothers, and friends, but Carolyn lost confidants and role models for how to live a fun, free, loving life based in self-worth and empowerment.

Carolyn took their example and began her own life with the same passion and drive she had seen in her grandmothers. As she grew into adulthood, got married and became a mother, she experienced the trials and tribulations that many of us do, and many experiences most of us hopefully never will.

From raising two teenage women to surviving domestic violence and ultimately divorcing and forging out on her own, Carolyn has come out the other side a stronger, more empathetic woman. As she continues her life-long journey of healing and self-reflection, she has realized her greatest accomplishment has been learning to love and forgive herself through it all.

Realizing this and doing something about her lack of self-love was a bigger challenge than she thought. Like many, Carolyn began her journey towards self-love by thinking it was about a new job, new home, and a decent splash of self-confidence. After extensive research and practicing everything she had learned, Carolyn began to experience the real benefit of self-love. After significant changes to her own life and happiness, Carolyn is now committed to helping other women embrace themselves and feel empowered.

JOIN US ON FACEBOOK

Join Our Facebook Community by following CCG Publishing!

By joining our page, you'll discover more easy-to-implement practices to help you cultivate self-love immediately.

We post things like:
- How to shift your mindset to focus on self-love and acceptance
- Simple daily practices that will help you stay connected to your self-worth
- How to let go of toxic relationships and surround yourself with positive influences

Plus, when you follow our page, you'll also receive exclusive access to free chapters from future e-books, hear from other women about their journeys, and tap into a community of self-love and empowerment!

Join us now to start your journey toward greater self-love and acceptance!

Discovering who you really are is a journey that requires self-reflection, self-love, and self-care. It is a process that involves looking inward, exploring your thoughts and feelings, and understanding your values and beliefs. Self-love is the foundation of this journey, as it enables you to appreciate and accept yourself for who you are. It also helps you to let go of negative self-talk and embrace positive affirmations that empower you to be your best self.

Women empowerment is another essential aspect of discovering who you really are. As a woman, you may have faced societal pressures and expectations that have influenced your self-perception. However, it is crucial to recognize that you have the power to define yourself on your own terms. By embracing your strengths, talents, and passions, you can empower yourself to pursue your dreams and live a fulfilling life.

Self-care is also crucial in discovering who you really are. Taking care of your physical, emotional, and mental well-being is essential to living a balanced life. Self-care practices such as exercise, meditation, and journaling can help you to connect with yourself on a deeper level, understand your needs, and cultivate a sense of inner peace and happiness.

How can we practice self-love?

Self-love is crucial for personal empowerment, and it's essential to practice self-care regularly. Women often overlook their needs, putting others' needs first and neglecting their well-being. To practice self-love, women must prioritize themselves and their needs. It's about accepting yourself, flaws and all, and treating yourself with kindness and compassion. It's about setting boundaries, saying no when needed, and taking time for yourself.

Self-care is also an integral part of self-love. It's about caring for your physical, emotional, and mental health. It's about eating well, exercising regularly, getting enough sleep, and caring for your skin and hair. It's also about doing things that make you happy and relaxed, like reading a book, taking a bubble bath, or walking.

Practicing self-love also means letting go of negative self-talk and limiting beliefs. It's about acknowledging your strengths, celebrating your accomplishments, and accepting your imperfections. It's about being kind to yourself, forgiving yourself, and learning from your mistakes.

Additionally, women can practice self-love by surrounding themselves with positive people and engaging in activities that bring them joy. It's about spending time with loved ones, pursuing hobbies and interests, and exploring new experiences. These actions help us accept ourselves, accept our emotions, and prioritize our physical, emotional, and mental well-being. When we remind ourselves that we deserve to be taken care of, we are more likely to make choices that nourish our well-being and serve us well.

Why don't women practice self-love?

The concept of self-love is a tricky one, and unfortunately, it is often more challenging for women to love themselves than it is for men. Many factors contribute to this difficulty, including societal expectations, personal experiences, and cultural norms. Women are often expected to be caretakers and to put the needs of others before their own, leading to a lack of self-care and self-love. Additionally, women are often judged more harshly for their appearance, leading to body image issues and a lack of confidence.

Personal experiences can also play a significant role in a woman's ability to love herself. Trauma, abuse, and neglect can all lead to feelings of unworthiness and low self-esteem. These experiences can make it challenging to see oneself as worthy of love and care.

Cultural norms can also contribute to the difficulty women face when it comes to self-love. In many cultures, women are expected to be modest, humble, and self-effacing. These expectations can make it challenging to acknowledge one's strengths and accomplishments and to feel deserving of self-love. Additionally, cultural messages about what it means to be a "good" woman can lead to feelings of guilt and shame when women prioritize their own needs and desires.

Despite the challenges, it is essential for women to learn to love themselves. Self-love is the foundation for healthy relationships, personal growth, and overall well-being. It is not always easy, but it is possible with practice and support. Women can start by focusing on self-care, setting boundaries, and challenging negative self-talk. Surrounding oneself with positive role models and seeking therapy or counseling can also be helpful in learning to love oneself.

What path brought you here?

In a world that is so connected through technology, it is essential to take time to reflect on our experiences. Reflection is the key to gaining insight into our own lives and creating a system that will serve us better in the future. While these questions are just guides to unlocking deep, powerful reflection, the key is to look within yourself to examine what experiences you've had - both good and bad - that made you the person you are today. Answering these types of questions allows us to gain a greater understanding of ourselves and our goals. Reflection is tiring, but it is essential to living a meaningful life. By taking time to reflect, we better understand ourselves and get closer to living our dream life.

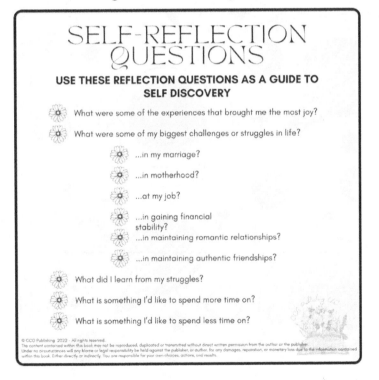

SELF-REFLECTION QUESTIONS

USE THESE REFLECTION QUESTIONS AS A GUIDE TO SELF DISCOVERY

What were some of the experiences that brought me the most joy?

What were some of my biggest challenges or struggles in life?

...in my marriage?

...in motherhood?

...at my job?

...in gaining financial stability?

...in maintaining romantic relationships?

...in maintaining authentic friendships?

What did I learn from my struggles?

What is something I'd like to spend more time on?

What is something I'd like to spend less time on?

Put it in practice: Who are you?

Taking time to reflect on who we are is crucial for personal growth and development. It allows us to understand our values, beliefs, and behaviors and how they shape our lives. Examining ourselves helps us recognize our strengths and weaknesses and identify areas for self-improvement. This process can be uncomfortable and challenging, but it is essential for our well-being and happiness.

30 DAYS OF REFLECTION

DAILY WRITING PROMPTS FOR SELF-DISCOVERY

1. What are your core values, and how do they influence your decisions?
2. What are your biggest fears, and how do they hold you back?
3. What are your goals for the next five years, and how do you plan to achieve them?
4. What motivates you, and how do you stay motivated?
5. What are your strengths, and how do you use them to your advantage?
6. What are your weaknesses, and how do you work on improving them?
7. What makes you happy, and how do you incorporate those things into your life?
8. Who are the people that have had the most significant impact on your life, and how have they influenced you?
9. What is your biggest regret, and what have you learned from it?
10. What is your biggest accomplishment, and how did you achieve it?
11. What are your hobbies, and how do they bring you joy?
12. What is your favorite memory, and why is it significant to you?
13. What are your pet peeves, and how do they affect your relationships?
14. What is your favorite book, and how has it influenced your life?
15. What is your favorite quote, and why does it resonate with you?
16. What is your favorite song, and how does it make you feel?
17. What is your favorite movie, and why do you love it?
18. What is your favorite food, and how does it make you feel when you eat it?
19. What makes you unique, and how do you embrace that?
20. What is your ideal day, and how can you make it a reality?
21. What are the things that stress you out, and how do you manage that stress?
22. What are your priorities in life, and how do you balance them?
23. What is your definition of success, and how do you measure it?
24. What is your definition of happiness, and how do you achieve it?
25. What are your thoughts on spirituality, and how do they influence your life?
26. What is your favorite place in the world, and why is it special to you?
27. What are your thoughts on love, and how do they impact your relationships?
28. What is your biggest pet peeve, and how do you cope with it?
29. What are your thoughts on forgiveness, and how do you practice it in your life?
30. What is your vision for your future, and how can you create it?

To encourage self-reflection, here are 30 writing prompts to explore who you are. Remember, self-discovery takes time, and revisiting your answers in a few days or weeks is okay. I recommend reflecting on one question per day and taking it as slowly as you need in order to get the most out of the process.

Not sure about journaling? It can be difficult to start, and maybe it feels a little awkward in the beginning to be writing down your thoughts and feelings. But the results speak for themselves if you put in the time! Lila, a young woman just out of college, was unsure about the true power of self-reflection and journaling, but she quickly realized the power of the practice.

In the days following her graduation from college, she noticed the excitement and joy faded more quickly than she expected. Of course, like many, she was stressed about finding a job, but the feelings she was experiencing were heavier than stress. She knew she'd find a job soon enough, and she had plenty saved to get her through. So what was it that was bringing her down? She spent several weeks writing and doodling in her journal in the evenings and in between interviews. She poured herself another glass of wine as she turned the page, and almost out of nowhere, she realized much of her heavy moods occurred when she was drinking.

Lila had always been a social drinker, but lately, it had become a daily habit. At first, she didn't think much of it. It helped her unwind after a long day of interviews, and she enjoyed the taste of wine. But soon enough, one glass turned into two, two turned into three, and before she knew it, the bottle was empty.

She tried to justify it to herself, saying that she deserved it after a hard day, but deep down, she knew it wasn't good for her. It wasn't until she took a step back and asked herself the difficult questions that she realized what was really going on. She was trying to fill a void in her life with alcohol. She didn't know what this void was or how to fill it, but she knew that drinking wasn't the answer. So she decided to face her fears head-on and seek the help she needed to overcome her addiction.

Next up: Killing Perfectionism

The first thing that will kill self-love is the idea that we have to be perfect. You will never indeed be able to love who you are if you can't accept that mistakes will be made. In the second chapter, we will work on overcoming perfectionism and learning to pivot so that you can achieve more.

CHAPTER 2

KILLING PERFECTIONISM

"At its root, perfectionism isn't really about a deep love of being meticulous. It's about fear. Fear of making a mistake. Fear of disappointing others. Fear of failure. Fear of success."
-Michael Law

Perfectionism is a trait that is often viewed in a positive light, as it is associated with high standards and achievement. However, when perfectionism becomes excessive and all-consuming, it can have negative consequences on an individual's mental and physical health. Unfortunately, studies show that perfectionism is more prevalent in women than in men.

Women are often socialized to prioritize the needs and expectations of others over their own. This can lead to a constant striving for perfection in order to meet societal expectations and avoid criticism or rejection. Additionally, women are held to higher standards and face more scrutiny in various aspects of life, including appearance, relationships, and career success.

The negative effects of perfectionism on women are numerous. Perfectionism can lead to anxiety, depression, and burnout, as individuals constantly feel pressure to meet impossible standards. It can also impact relationships, as perfectionists may struggle to accept imperfections in themselves and others. Furthermore, perfectionism can inhibit creativity and risk-taking, as individuals are afraid to make mistakes or fail.

What Perfectionism Is Doing to You

It is important for women to recognize the potential harm of perfectionism and to work towards a healthier relationship with striving for success. This includes acknowledging that perfection is unattainable, and that mistakes and failures are a natural part of growth and learning. Seeking support from loved ones, a therapist, or a support group can also be helpful in navigating the pressures of perfectionism. By embracing imperfection and focusing on self-acceptance and self-care, women can break free from the cycle of perfectionism and live a more fulfilling life.

Emily was a young artist living in New York City. She was a talented artist who strived for perfection in everything she did. She spent countless hours honing her craft, making sure every brushstroke was perfect and every color was just right. Her work was praised by many, and she was quickly becoming known as one of the best artists in her town.

However, as Emily's career began to take off, she started to notice that her perfectionism was taking a toll on her mental health. She would spend sleepless nights worrying about her art, constantly striving to make it better. Her relationships with her friends and family began to suffer, as she would cancel plans to work on her art.

One day, Emily had an epiphany. She realized that her pursuit of perfection was causing her more harm than good. She decided to take a step back and focus on enjoying the process of creating art rather than obsessing over the end result. She began to prioritize her mental health and started taking breaks when she needed them.

As Emily started to let go of her perfectionism, she found that her art became even better. She was able to experiment with new styles and techniques, and her work became more authentic and expressive. She found that her relationships with her loved ones improved, and she was able to enjoy life outside of her art.

In the end, Emily learned that perfectionism is not worth sacrificing your mental health and relationships. She found a healthier balance and was able to continue creating beautiful art while also enjoying life to the fullest.

The Truth About Mistakes

Most of us don't want to be wrong because the consequences can be severe, ranging from losing a job to jail time or even death. This feeling of being wrong is unpleasant and can make us feel humiliated, alienated, ashamed, insecure, vulnerable, and bewildered. The flip side is that being right is satisfying and can be very gratifying.

However, while we should always strive to be right, being wrong is an unavoidable part of life. Humans are prone to bias, irrationality, and naivete. The harm can come from not being open to the possibility of being wrong, as it is a necessary part of growth and success.

Kathryn Schultz's book, *Being Wrong: Adventures in the Margin of Error,* argues that embracing and being open to being wrong can improve our relationships, make us smarter and more creative, and make life more fun. We often believe we are right because of our upbringing, our parents, our communities, and our personal experiences, and not because of our own research. This can make it hard to change our minds when it's proven that we are wrong or that our beliefs are limited. However, intellectual threats can be seen in the same way as physical threats, as our beliefs provide security and safety in how we view the world.

Recognizing Past Mistakes and Finding Forgiveness

At times, we do or say things that we later regret. When this happens, it can be tough to forgive ourselves, especially if it involves someone we care about. I recently had a falling out with a friend that occurred quickly and unexpectedly. She was trying to get me to invest in a project alongside her, and I politely declined. When I felt she was coming off too pushy, I interpreted her words as an insult and responded with anger. After reflecting, I realized I had misread the situation and reacted too strongly. I feared our relationship would be irreparably damaged, and I was ashamed that I let my frustration and emotions get the best of me.

In situations like this, we have two main options. We can run away and hide, and hope it "blows over". Typically, when we take this road, we spent time embarrassed, ashamed, and generally being hard on ourselves for making a mistake. The second option is to admit we make a mistake, apologize to those involved, and apologize to ourselves. This option takes vulnerability and can be awkward at first, but ultimately its way easier in the long run, because it saves us time and emotion in feeling bad, running away, or letting relationships that were important to us fall to the side because of something we regret.

Forgiveness: A 7-Step Process

STEP ONE: Identify the actions that led to the incident. Write down the details and focus on yourself rather than blaming external people or circumstances. Acknowledge your vulnerability, but don't suppress it.

STEP TWO: Ask for forgiveness. It's difficult, but approach the person you hurt and take responsibility for your actions.

STEP THREE: Forgive yourself every time negative thoughts come into your head. Self-forgiveness is a process, so do something kind for yourself when these thoughts arise.

STEP FOUR: Show up and let yourself be seen. Don't run away or hide in shame. Even if you're afraid of being judged, trying again is important.

STEP FIVE: Be thankful for your mistakes. Think of them as opportunities to grow.

STEP SIX: Radically love all of yourself, mistakes included. Joseph Campbell said, "The privilege of a lifetime is being who you are," so embrace who you have become due to your past wrongs.

STEP SEVEN: Grow from your mistakes. Look to the future and use what you have learned to strengthen your relationships.

While my personal story above was one related to a close friend, reflection and personal forgiveness can be associated with both day-to-day interactions and experiences that span lifetimes.

One woman reflects on her experiences as a mother, who one day looked in the mirror and didn't recognize who she had become. She started reflecting on her experiences and the choices she made over the years and quickly fell into despair and anger at herself for forgetting how confident and full of life she used to be.

As she watched her children grow and thrive, the woman began to realize that she had lost touch with her sense of self-acceptance. She had spent too many years trying to fit into societal norms and striving for perfection, which had affected her mental health and well-being. But seeing her children's carefree and joyful nature reminded her of the importance of embracing herself for who she truly was.

She started to let go of her insecurities and started to appreciate her own unique qualities. She began to dance and sing with her children in the street, and soon, she found herself smiling and laughing more often. As she continued to embrace her true self, she became a role model for her children, showing them that it's important to love and accept themselves just the way they are.

Over time, the woman's self-confidence grew, and she pursued her passions and interests. She started taking art classes, which she had always wanted to do but had been too afraid to try. She even started her own business selling her artwork; her children were her biggest supporters.

Through the inspiration of her children, the woman found a new sense of purpose and happiness in her life. She learned that sometimes the best way to find self-acceptance is to look to those who love and accept us unconditionally and to forgive ourselves for the times we didn't measure up to our own expectations of ourselves.

Next up: Negative Thinking

Accepting that you are not perfect and will make mistakes requires one additional skill: **to rewire the brain.** Right now, you are probably bombarding yourself with negative thoughts about what went wrong and what could be better. It's time to start rephrasing these thoughts so that they are of use.

A negative mind can be a significant obstacle in our daily lives, causing stress, anxiety, and even depression. However, understanding why our brain leans towards negativity and implementing practical steps to transform negative thoughts into positive ones can help us regain control and improve our overall well-being. In this chapter, we will explore the reasons behind negative thinking and provide practical techniques to overcome it without forcing toxic positivity.

The Science Behind Negative Thinking

Why Our Brain Leans Towards Negativity

One of the primary reasons for our brain's inclination toward negativity is our evolutionary history. Our prehistoric ancestors relied on their ability to anticipate threats and dangers to ensure their survival. This ability to predict and react to potential hazards has been ingrained in our brains, making us more prone to focus on negative events and experiences.

Moreover, our negative thinking patterns can become habits over time, reinforced by the neural pathways we create. As we repeatedly engage in negative thoughts, these pathways become stronger, making it difficult for us to break free from these destructive cycles.

The Impact of Negative Thoughts on Our Brain

Chronic negative thinking can have detrimental effects on our brain and overall mental health. It can deplete essential brain chemicals like serotonin and dopamine, which are responsible for regulating our moods and emotions. Additionally, it can weaken the production of brain-derived neurotrophic factor (BDNF), a protein necessary for new brain cell formation.

Negative thoughts can also shrink the size of our brain while enlarging the amygdala, the brain's fear center, increasing our susceptibility to psychiatric and neurodegenerative diseases. Furthermore, persistent negative thinking can accelerate the brain's aging process, making it crucial for us to regain control over our thoughts and emotions.

Automatic Negative Thoughts (ANTs)

Automatic Negative Thoughts (ANTs) are negative thoughts that come to our minds automatically and without any conscious effort. These thoughts are usually negative and can be about ourselves, others, or the world in general. ANTs can be very damaging to our mental and emotional well-being, as they can lead to feelings of anxiety, depression, and low self-esteem.

But why is it that so many of us are prone to negative thinking? One of the main reasons is our evolutionary history. Our brains are wired to detect and respond to threats in the environment, and negative thoughts can be a way of preparing us for danger. This is known as the negativity bias, and it is a natural tendency that has helped us survive as a species. So even though it is a frustrating behavior, it is completely natural and rooted in our DNA!

Another reason why humans are prone to negative thinking is due to our past experiences. Negative experiences can leave a lasting impression on our minds, and we may develop negative beliefs or thought patterns as a result.

Additionally, societal and cultural factors can also contribute to negative thinking. We are constantly bombarded with messages of perfectionism and unrealistic expectations, which can lead us to feel inadequate or like we are not enough. Social comparison is also a common practice, and we may compare ourselves to others and feel like we don't measure up.

It's important to note that while negative thoughts are natural, they don't have to control our lives. We can learn to challenge and reframe our negative thoughts through practices such as cognitive-behavioral therapy (CBT), mindfulness, and positive psychology, all topics we'll cover in future chapters. By learning how to recognize and manage our ANTs, we can improve our mental health and overall well-being.

Types of Automatic Negative Thoughts

All or Nothing. The first category of ANTs is the "All or Nothing" thinking, where an individual thinks in extremes. For instance, thinking that everything is either black or white and there are no shades of gray. This kind of thinking can lead to unrealistic expectations and disappointment.

Overgeneralizations. The second category is "Overgeneralization," where one takes a single negative experience and applies it to all situations.

For example, if someone fails in one job interview, they may start believing that they will never get a job.

Mental Filters The third category of ANTs is the "Mental Filter," where an individual focuses only on the negative aspects of a situation and ignores the positive aspects. This kind of thinking can lead to a distorted view of reality and relationships can suffer. For example, focusing on one negative piece of feedback from a review and ignoring the other positive pieces of feedback is a type of mental filter.

Discounting Positives. The fourth category is "Discounting the Positive," where an individual ignores or dismisses positive experiences and only focuses on the negative. For example, if someone receives a compliment, they may dismiss it by saying that the other person was just being polite.

Jumping to Conclusions. The fifth category is "Jumping to Conclusions," where an individual makes negative assumptions without any evidence. For instance, assuming that someone is angry with you because they did not reply to your text message.

Exaggerations. The sixth category is "Magnification and Minimization," where an individual exaggerates the negative aspects of a situation and minimizes the positive aspects. This kind of thinking can lead to feelings of hopelessness and despair.

Emotional Reasoning. Finally, the seventh category is "Emotional Reasoning," where an individual believes that their emotions reflect reality. For instance, feeling anxious about a situation and assuming that it must be dangerous.

Do any of these Automatic Negative Thoughts sound like you? You aren't alone! It can be frustrating when our minds automatically focus on the negative, but the more we learn about these types of behaviors and why we have them, the better we'll be at changing how we think and feel. Overall, ANTs are unproductive and repetitive thought patterns that can significantly impact our mental health, and becoming aware of these patterns can be the first step towards cultivating a more positive and productive mindset. Let's explore ways we can identify our own ANTs in the moment, and work towards diverting these thoughts or reframing them into positives.

Identifying Our ANTs

The first step in identifying ANTs is to become aware of them. Pay attention to your thoughts and identify the ones that make you feel anxious, upset, or angry. Once you become aware of these thoughts, you can start to challenge them. Ask yourself if they are true or if they are just assumptions or interpretations. Often, our negative thoughts are not based on reality but rather on our perceptions of reality.

Another useful tactic in identifying ANTs is to keep a journal. Write down your thoughts regularly and review them later. This will help you identify patterns in your thinking and recognize your ANTs more easily. It will also give you the opportunity to challenge your negative thoughts and replace them with positive ones. It is important to remember that identifying ANTs takes time and practice. Be patient with yourself, and don't give up if you don't see immediate results. Remember that every small step you take towards identifying and challenging your negative thoughts is progress toward a healthier mindset.

Identifying Automatic Negative Thoughts is an important step toward improving your mental health and well-being. By becoming aware of your negative thoughts, challenging them, and replacing them with positive ones, you can improve your mood, reduce anxiety, and improve your overall quality of life. So take the time to identify your ANTs and start working towards a happier, healthier you.

More Ways to Get Rid of ANTs

1. Ask yourself questions. When you notice an ANT, challenge its validity by asking yourself to help you gain perspective and realize that there are alternative ways to view the situation.

-Is this thought true?

-Does having this thought serve me?

-Is there another explanation or another way of looking at things?

-What advice would I give to a friend who had this thought?

2. Write down your automatic negative thoughts. By writing down your ANTs, you can identify patterns in your thinking and discover triggers for these thoughts. This insight can help you feel less overwhelmed and better equipped to tackle your negative thinking patterns.

3. Personify Your Inner Critic. Visualizing your inner critic as an external entity, such as a devil on your shoulder or an "evil twin," can help you distance yourself from these thoughts and prevent them from consuming you. Remind yourself that this voice does not have your best interests at heart and should not be taken seriously.

4. View your negative thoughts as boring. Instead of engaging with your negative thoughts, try viewing them as uninteresting and repetitive. Recognize that not every thought you have is important or true and allow these thoughts to pass without giving them too much attention.

5. Turn your ANTs into Positive Empowering Thoughts (PETs). Reframe your negative thoughts into more uplifting and realistic alternatives, known as PETs. This process involves transforming statements like "I should" or "I shouldn't" into more positive phrases that focus on benefits or alignment with your values.

6. Reframe "should" and "shouldn't" statements. Replace "should" and "shouldn't" statements with more positive phrases that focus on the benefits of an action or its alignment with your values. For example, instead of saying, "I should exercise," tell yourself, "I look forward to exercising," or "I love the way I feel after I exercise."

When to Consider Professional Help for Negative Thoughts

If you feel overwhelmed by negative thoughts, or if they significantly impact your daily life, consider seeking professional help. Cognitive-behavioral therapy (CBT) is a popular and effective approach to addressing negative thought patterns and improving overall mental health. Working with a trained therapist can help you uncover the root causes of your negative thinking and develop strategies for overcoming it.

Calming and controlling the negative mind is essential for our overall well-being and happiness. By understanding the reasons behind our brain's inclination towards negativity and implementing practical steps to transform negative thoughts into positive ones, we can regain control over our thoughts and emotions, avoiding the pitfalls of toxic positivity. With persistence and practice, we can cultivate a more balanced and positive mindset, leading to a happier and healthier life.

Thoughts and emotions are so closely knitted that it's often hard to see where one ends and another begins. In the next chapter, we will discover the role of emotional intelligence in self-love.

Toxic Positivity

On the complete opposite side of the spectrum is toxic positivity, a phenomenon where people ignore or suppress negative emotions and thoughts in order to maintain a positive outlook on life. While it is important to strive for positivity and optimism, it is equally important to acknowledge and process negative emotions. Toxic positivity can be harmful because it can invalidate someone's feelings and lead to a lack of empathy.

One of the most common examples of toxic positivity is the phrase "positive vibes only." This phrase suggests that negative emotions are not welcome, and that people should only focus on positive things. Unfortunately, life is not always positive, and ignoring negative emotions can be damaging in the long run. This type of toxic positivity can make people feel like they're not allowed to express their true feelings and can create a culture of emotional repression.

Another example of toxic positivity is the idea that "it could always be worse." While it's true that things could always be worse, this type of thinking can be dismissive of someone's struggles and make them feel like their problems aren't valid. It's important to acknowledge that everyone's experiences are different and that just because someone else has it worse doesn't mean that your own struggles are insignificant.

Taming Our Toxic Positivity

So how can we stop toxic positivity? First, we need to recognize when we're engaging in this behavior. If you find yourself dismissing someone's feelings or telling them to "just think positively," take a step back and try to empathize with them instead. Listen to what they're saying and validate their emotions.

Secondly, we need to create a culture where it's okay to express negative emotions. Encourage open communication and let people know that it's okay to be vulnerable. This will allow for a more authentic and empathetic environment. Give yourself the same permission to feel negative thoughts, feel them, and release them.

Lastly, we need to remember that positivity doesn't mean ignoring negativity. It's okay to acknowledge negative emotions and work through them in order to grow and learn from our experiences. By embracing both positive and negative emotions, we can create a more balanced and healthy approach to life.

Overthinking

Overthinking is a common problem that many of us face at some point in our lives. It is a state where we tend to dwell on a single thought or a situation for a prolonged period, often leading to anxiety, stress, and confusion. Overthinking can be caused by various reasons such as past traumas, future uncertainties, or any other triggers that may cause our mind to spiral out of control. If you're someone who is struggling with overthinking, you're not alone. The good news is that there are several ways to stop overthinking and regain control of your mind.

Ways to Curb Overthinking

Practice Mindfulness. Mindfulness is the practice of being present in the moment and focusing on your thoughts and feelings without judgment. When you practice mindfulness, you can observe your thoughts and emotions without becoming attached to them. This allows you to gain clarity and distance from your thoughts, making it easier to let go of them. We'll discuss mindfulness practices in great detail in Chapter 11.

Challenge Your Thoughts. When you find yourself overthinking, try to challenge your thoughts by asking yourself questions like, "Is this thought based on facts or assumptions?", "What evidence do I have to support this thought?", "What's the worst that could happen if this thought came true?" Challenging your thoughts can help you gain perspective and reduce the intensity of your emotions.

Take Action. Overthinking often leads to inaction, which further reinforces our negative thoughts. To break this cycle, try taking small steps towards addressing the situation that's causing you to overthink. Even if the steps are small, taking action can give you a sense of control and help you feel more confident in your ability to handle the situation.

Distract Yourself. Sometimes, the best way to stop overthinking is to distract yourself with something else. Engage in an activity that requires your full attention, such as reading a book, going for a walk, or doing a puzzle. This can help you shift your focus away from your thoughts and give your mind a break. In conclusion, overthinking can be a challenging problem to deal with, but it's not impossible to overcome.

By practicing mindfulness, challenging your thoughts, taking action, and distracting yourself, you can regain control of your mind and reduce the negative impact of overthinking on your mental health. Remember that it's okay to seek professional help if you're struggling to cope with overthinking on your own.

Next up: Understanding Our Emotions

Thoughts and emotions are so closely knitted that it's often hard to see where one ends and another begins. In the next chapter, we will discover the role of emotional intelligence in self-love.

CHAPTER 4

GETTING COMFORTABLE WITH YOUR EMOTIONS

"Somehow, it seems that the sadder a song is, the happier I feel. The release of emotions that many would label as 'negative' is actually a liberating process for me."
- Grey DeLisle

Emotions are an integral part of our lives, influencing our thoughts, decisions, and actions. While society often promotes the idea that some emotions are "good" and others are "bad," it's essential to understand and embrace the full spectrum of our emotional experiences. In this chapter we focus on ways we can break free from the stereotypical idea that women are emotional, and men are angry, and discover why all emotions are essential and exist for a reason. We'll also provide step-by-step activities to improve your emotional awareness and learn how to stop letting emotions get the better of you.

The Purpose of Emotions

Emotions serve various purposes in our lives, from motivating us to make difficult decisions to help us maintain meaningful relationships. They enable us to connect with others on a deeper level and navigate the complexities of the world around us. Understanding and embracing all emotions, including those deemed as negative, can lead to increased self-awareness, empathy, and resilience.

All emotions, whether comfortable or not, provide valuable information about our wants, needs, and experiences. Reflecting on *how* emotions arise within our everyday lives can strengthen our social and emotional competence. Emotions like joy, for instance, give us a sense of purpose and well-being, while more challenging emotions like disgust help us redirect what is harmful or unhealthy. As we become more aware of the purpose behind our emotions, we can better manage both positive and challenging situations.

Just like avoiding both ANTs and toxic positivity in Chapter 3, it is equally crucial to recognize and accept all emotions, whether they are positive or negative. Avoiding or suppressing certain emotions can lead to decreased well-being and increased physical symptoms of stress, such as headaches. On the other hand, acknowledging and addressing our feelings allows us to develop insights, create a roadmap to address problems, and ultimately enhance our overall well-being.

Broadening Your Emotional Vocabulary

To get more comfortable with all of your emotions, it's helpful to expand your emotional vocabulary. It sounds simple, but naming emotions can be harder than you think! This practice involves finding and using more precise and nuanced words to describe your feelings. By doing so, you can more accurately identify and address the emotions you're experiencing.

Have you ever wondered what a particular emotion is called? How do you categorize your feelings? It's one of those questions that you wouldn't come with on your own, but once it's asked, it's impossible not to think about.

The first time this came up for me was after meeting a fellow writer, Tanya. She and I were very similar, but she was also so different in a way I couldn't understand at first. She had this incredible ability to articulate how she felt. Whether it was frustration, happiness, or sadness, Tanya could describe her emotions with such accuracy and precision that it was almost poetic.

I was intrigued, so I asked her how she did it. She explained that it all had to do with naming her emotions. She had this little notebook where she wrote down how she felt every day and what triggered those emotions. Over time, she began to notice patterns and could identify specific feelings more easily.

Fast forward a few months, and I decided to try it out for myself. At first, it was awkward, and I found myself struggling to put my emotions into words. But with practice, it became easier. I found that naming my emotions gave me a sense of control over them. I could identify what was causing me to feel a certain way and could take steps to either change my situation or my reaction to it.

Now, I can confidently say that naming my emotions has transformed my life. I feel more connected to my feelings, and I've gained a deeper understanding of myself. I'm no longer a skeptic. Instead, I'm a believer in the power of naming your emotions and doing something about them.

Emotional Intelligence is Key to Self-Love

Emotional intelligence, also known as EI, emotional quotient, or EQ, is the ability to understand, use, and manage your own emotions in positive ways to relieve stress, communicate effectively, empathize with others, overcome challenges, and defuse conflict. Developing emotional intelligence involves cultivating self-awareness, self-management, social awareness, and relationship management.

When we have a good level of emotional intelligence, we are better equipped to identify our own needs and take care of ourselves, which is an essential aspect of self-love. Emotional intelligence involves several skills, including self-awareness, self-regulation, empathy, and social skills.

Self-Awareness

Self-awareness refers to our ability to recognize and understand our own emotions, thoughts, and behaviors. When we have a high level of self-awareness, we are better able to identify our needs and desires, as well as our strengths and weaknesses. This allows us to make better decisions for ourselves and take actions that align with our values.

Have you ever been around someone who is painfully un-self-aware? Did that question immediately make you think of someone you know and dread being around? For me, this is a previous colleague named Sarah. I worked with her for years and dreaded being in meetings with her, because it was impossible to get a word in. The minute any of us tried to make a point, Sarah would jump back into the conversation before two words left our mouth.

One day, Sarah was sitting at her desk, scrolling through her social media feed, not realizing that she was running late for her meeting. For the last few years, she had been struggling to make friends, and her career growth had been stunted. It seemed like she was always making the wrong impression, saying the wrong thing, or just not being self-aware enough. Despite these challenges, Sarah had never really considered that she might be the problem.

The tragic thing about Sarah is that she actually had a lot to offer. She was smart and capable, but somehow it seemed like no one ever saw that. The meeting was going well, and Sarah was starting to feel more confident. She was presenting some ideas to the team, and everyone was nodding along, but then something strange happened. One of our colleagues spoke up and said, "Sarah, do you realize how often you interrupt people?"

Sarah was clearly taken aback. She had never realized that she did that. But as she thought back on all the times that she had tried to join in on conversations, she realized that it was true. She was always interrupting people, and it was making them feel like she wasn't really listening to them. She felt ashamed and embarrassed as she left the meeting.

Over the next few weeks, Sarah made a conscious effort to be more aware of how she was communicating with others. She started listening more and interrupting less. And to her surprise, she started making connections with people. Our colleagues started seeking her out for advice and input on projects. And even outside of work, Sarah found that she was making new friends.

Looking back, Sarah realized that she had been her own worst enemy. She had been so focused on what she wanted to say that she hadn't been really hearing what others had to say. But now that she was more self-aware, she was finally able to connect with people on a deeper level. And as she looked to the future, she knew that she would never stop striving to be the best version of herself.

Self-Regulation

Self-regulation is the ability to manage our own emotions and behaviors effectively. When we are emotionally intelligent, we can regulate our emotions in a healthy way, rather than being controlled by them. This means that we can respond to situations calmly and thoughtfully, rather than impulsively. This is a key aspect of self-love because it allows us to prioritize self-care and avoid self-destructive behaviors.

Empathy

Empathy is the ability to understand and share the feelings of others. When we are empathetic, we can connect with others on a deeper level and build stronger relationships. This is important for self-love because it helps us recognize the importance of connection and support from others in our lives.

Social Skills

These are the skills we use to interact with others effectively. When we have strong social skills, we can communicate clearly and assertively, set healthy boundaries, and build positive relationships. This is important for self-love because it allows us to advocate for ourselves and build supportive networks.

Emotional intelligence is key to self-love because it allows us to understand and manage our own emotions, as well as the emotions of others. By developing our emotional intelligence skills, we can prioritize self-care, regulate our emotions effectively, build strong relationships, and advocate for ourselves. This ultimately leads to greater self-love and a more fulfilling life.

Getting comfortable with all of your emotions requires recognizing their importance, challenging stereotypes, and developing strategies to manage them effectively. Embracing the full spectrum of emotions can enhance your self-awareness, forge deeper connections with others, and lead a more fulfilling life.

Next up: Toxic Relationships

What emotions are stirred up when you think about the people in your life? Do the people in your life love you for who you are or because of the person you were? Will they still be around when you make self-love a priority? Toxic people come in all shapes and sizes but if there is one thing they have in common, they won't hesitate to drain you of all your strength.

Toxic relationships are detrimental to your mental, emotional, and physical well-being. They can leave you feeling drained, unhappy, and even insecure about yourself. In this chapter, we will outline what toxic relationships look like, explore people-pleasing behavior and assertiveness, and discuss how to handle toxic people and when it's time to remove them from your life. Ultimately these practices will help you recognize and overcome toxic relationships, enabling you to live a healthier and more fulfilling life and continue your self-love journey.

Recognizing Toxic Relationships

Before we can address the issue of toxic relationships, it's crucial to understand what they look like. Toxic relationships come in many forms and can involve various types of manipulation, control, and emotional abuse. Women coming out of bad divorces, widows, people who only know toxic relationships as the norm or women – how can we avoid these toxic relationships in the future and break the cycles of toxicity?

Spotting toxic relationships can be difficult, especially if you are emotionally invested in the relationship. However, there are some red flags that can help you identify a toxic relationship. Firstly, if your partner is controlling and manipulative, this can be a major sign of toxicity. Do they try to isolate you from your family and friends? Do they make decisions without consulting you? These are warning signs that your partner is trying to control you.

Secondly, if your partner is constantly criticizing you or putting you down, this can be a sign of a toxic relationship. A healthy relationship should be built on mutual respect and support, not constant criticism.

Thirdly, if your partner is emotionally abusive, this is a major red flag. Emotional abuse can take many forms, such as verbal abuse, gaslighting, or withholding affection as a form of punishment.

Common Signs of a Toxic Relationship

Constant Criticism. In a toxic relationship, one partner may constantly criticize the other, focusing on their flaws and shortcomings. This can lead to feelings of inadequacy and low self-esteem in the person being criticized.

Jealousy and Control. A toxic partner may exhibit excessive jealousy and try to control their partner's actions, friends, or even appearance. This can create a suffocating environment where the person being controlled feels trapped and powerless.

Lack of Support. In a healthy relationship, partners support each other's goals, dreams, and aspirations. In a toxic relationship, one partner may undermine or dismiss the other's achievements, leaving them feeling unsupported and undervalued.

Emotional Manipulation. Toxic partners may use emotional manipulation tactics, such as guilt-tripping, to get their way. They may also play the victim, making their partner feel responsible for their well-being and happiness.

Constant Drama. Toxic relationships can be characterized by constant drama and conflict, leaving both partners feeling emotionally drained and exhausted.

Have you ever found yourself in a relationship that leaves you feeling drained, hopeless, and confused? You're not alone. A lot of people struggle with identifying toxic relationships and finding a way out of them, but, the good news is that it's never too late to make a change.

Samantha was a successful copywriter who took pride in her work. However, her personal life was nowhere near as fulfilling. She found herself in a relationship that was slowly chipping away at her confidence. Her partner constantly belittled her work, made her feel inadequate, and never took her opinions seriously. It drained her of her creativity and left her feeling disillusioned.

Samantha knew this wasn't the kind of relationship she deserved but had no idea how to get out of it. She would talk to her friends, but they would tell her to 'just leave' which was easier said than done. But one day, she decided enough was enough. She started researching how to identify toxic relationships and found a wealth of information that helped her come to terms with her situation.

Through her research, Samantha learned that toxic relationships often leave us feeling like we can't live without our partner. The truth is, we're better off without someone who brings us down. It's important to remember that you are deserving of love, respect, and kindness.

Samantha took the courageous step of ending her relationship and moving on. Though difficult at first, she was soon able to channel all the energy she had lost into her work, and her creativity was back better than ever. By taking the time to identify toxic relationships and finding a way to get out of them, Samantha was able to regain control of her life.

The power of identifying toxic relationships and finding a way out of them cannot be overstated. If you're in a similar situation to Samantha, remember that you are not alone, and that there is always a way out. Take the step, learn to love and respect yourself, and you will find happiness.

Ending Toxic Relationships

Knowing when to remove toxic people from your life can be a difficult decision, but it's an important one for your mental and emotional well-being. Once you've recognized the signs of toxic relationships, it's crucial to know how to handle toxic people and when it's time to remove them from your life.

They constantly bring negativity into your life

If someone is always complaining, gossiping, or criticizing others, it can wear you down over time. Negativity breeds negativity, and being around someone who always has something negative to say can start to affect your own mindset.

They don't respect your boundaries

Toxic people often push past boundaries and don't respect your needs or wants. If someone is constantly crossing your boundaries, it's a sign that they don't value or respect you as a person.

They drain your energy.

Have you ever felt exhausted after spending time with someone? That's a sign that they may be draining your energy. Toxic people often demand a lot of attention and emotional labor, leaving you feeling drained and depleted.

They are manipulative or controlling.

Manipulative people will often try to control your actions or decisions, whether it's through guilt-tripping, gaslighting, or other tactics. If someone is trying to control you or manipulate you, it's a sign that they don't have your best interests at heart.

They don't take responsibility for their actions.

Toxic people often blame others for their problems and refuse to take responsibility for their own actions. If someone is always deflecting blame onto others, it's a sign that they are not willing to grow or change.

If you notice these signs in someone in your life, it may be time to consider removing them from your life. It's important to prioritize your own well-being and surround yourself with people who lift you up and support you.

However, removing toxic people from your life can be easier said than done. If the person is a family member or close friend, it may be more complicated. In these cases, it's important to set boundaries and communicate your needs clearly. If the person is unwilling to respect your boundaries or make changes, it may be necessary to limit your interaction with them. Make a plan safety plan and ensure you have support from family and friends who are also in the loop about your plan to end these relationships.

Remember, you deserve to be surrounded by positive and supportive people who add value to your life. Don't be afraid to make the tough decision to remove toxic people from your life if it's necessary for your own happiness and well-being. Recognizing and overcoming toxic relationships is crucial for your overall well-being. By understanding the signs of toxic relationships, developing assertiveness skills, and learning to handle toxic people effectively, you can create a healthier, more fulfilling life for yourself. Remember, you undeniably deserve more than toxic relationships, and it's never too late to make a change for the better.

Important: A Note About Domestic Violence

For anyone in a toxic relationship that has led to domestic violence, your safety is important. Help is available at from the National Domestic Violence Hotline at 800-799-7233.

First and foremost, it's important to acknowledge how brave you are for recognizing that you are in an abusive relationship and seeking help. Getting out of an abusive relationship can be a difficult and scary process, but it's important to prioritize your safety and well-being above all else. Here are some steps you can take to safely end the relationship:

Create a safety plan: Before taking any action, create a plan to ensure your safety. This should include identifying a safe place to go, packing a bag with essentials, and having a list of emergency contacts. The time you leave, and the days leading up to and following it, are the most dangerous.

Seek support: It's important to have a support system in place before leaving the relationship. Reach out to friends, family members or a domestic violence hotline for emotional support and guidance.

Document the abuse: Keep a record of any incidents of abuse, including dates, times, and details of what happened. This may be useful if you decide to seek legal action.

Contact a professional: Consider reaching out to a therapist or counselor who specializes in domestic violence to help you process your emotions and develop coping strategies.

End the relationship: When you are ready to end the relationship, do so in a public place or with someone you trust present. Be firm and clear in your communication and avoid engaging in arguments or discussions about the relationship.

Secure your safety: Change your phone number, block your ex-partner on social media and consider getting a restraining order if necessary.

Remember that leaving an abusive relationship is not easy and may take time. It's important to prioritize your safety and well-being throughout the process. Don't hesitate to seek support from professionals who can guide you through this difficult time.

People Pleasing vs. Toxic Relationships

People pleasing is a common behavior where an individual prioritizes the wants and needs of others over their own. It can stem from a desire to be liked or accepted, fear of rejection or conflict, or a need for validation. People pleasers often struggle with setting boundaries, saying "no," and asserting their own needs.

On the other hand, toxic relationships are characterized by behaviors that are harmful or abusive. This can include verbal or physical abuse, manipulation, gaslighting, and controlling behavior.

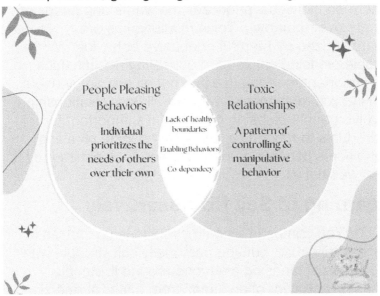

People Pleasing Behaviors — Individual prioritizes the needs of others over their own

Lack of healthy boundaries — Enabling Behaviors — Co dependecy

Toxic Relationships — A pattern of controlling & manipulative behavior

Toxic relationships can have a significant impact on an individual's mental and emotional well-being, and it's important to recognize the signs and seek help if necessary.

While people pleasing can lead to unhealthy relationships, it's important to note that not all people pleasers are in toxic relationships and not all toxic relationships involve people pleasing behavior. It's possible for individuals to engage in people pleasing behavior without being in a toxic relationship, and it's possible for individuals in toxic relationships to not engage in people pleasing behavior.

It's important for individuals to recognize when their people pleasing behavior is becoming unhealthy and to work on setting healthy boundaries. This can involve learning to say "no," prioritizing self-care, and seeking support from friends, family, or a therapist.

In summary, people pleasing is a behavior where an individual prioritizes the wants and needs of others over their own. Toxic relationships are characterized by harmful or abusive behaviors. While people pleasing can lead to unhealthy relationships, it's important to recognize that not all people pleasers are in toxic relationships and not all toxic relationships involve people pleasing behavior. It's important for individuals to recognize when their people pleasing behavior is becoming unhealthy and to prioritize their own well-being.

Learning to Say No Assertively

You can be in a healthy relationship that isn't necessarily toxic, but you personally still struggle with the stress of pleasing everyone around it. People-pleasing behavior often stems from a fear of rejection or a desire to be liked by others. This can lead to difficulty saying no and setting boundaries in relationships. And most importantly, saying yes to everything can lead to burnout, resentment, and feeling overwhelmed, like my good friend Anna experienced.

Anna had always been a people pleaser. From a young age, she was taught to avoid conflict and to prioritize making others happy. As she grew older, this trait followed her into her personal and professional life. She found herself constantly saying "yes" to everyone and everything, even when it meant sacrificing her own needs and desires.

But as time went on, Anna began to feel drained and resentful. She realized that her constant need to please others was actually holding her back from living the life she wanted. So, she decided to make a change.

Anna began to set boundaries and say "no" when she needed to. At first, it was hard. She worried that people would be angry or disappointed with her. But to her surprise, most people respected her assertiveness and admired her for standing up for herself.

As she became more confident in her ability to say no, Anna noticed a shift in her life. She no longer felt burdened by the expectations of others, and she had more time and energy to pursue her own goals and passions. She started a side business and began to take risks she never would have before.

Now, Anna looks back on her people-pleasing days with a sense of gratitude. She knows that they taught her how to be compassionate and empathetic, but she also knows that it's important to prioritize her own needs and desires. And she encourages others to do the same to unlock a whole new world of possibilities.

Tips for Overcoming People Pleasing Behaviors

Identify your values and priorities. Knowing what's important to you the first step is in setting boundaries and saying no. If you're not clear on your values and priorities, it's easy to get caught up in pleasing others and neglecting your own needs.

Practice saying no. Saying no can be uncomfortable at first, but like any skill, it gets easier with practice.

Start by saying no to small requests and work your way up to more significant commitments. Saying no can be challenging for people-pleasers, but it's essential for establishing boundaries and maintaining self-respect. Practice saying no without offering lengthy explanations or excuses.

Use "I" statements. When you say no, use "I" statements instead of "you" statements. For example, instead of saying, "You're asking too much of me," say, "I don't have the bandwidth to take on any more projects right now."

Set boundaries. Establish clear boundaries with others about what you're willing and able to do. Communicate your boundaries clearly and consistently.

Offer alternatives. When possible, offer alternatives to saying yes or no. For example, if someone asks you to attend a social event that you don't want to go to, suggest meeting up for coffee or lunch instead. Assertiveness involves finding a compromise that meets both parties needs. Learn to negotiate and be willing to make adjustments to reach a mutually beneficial solution.

Be confident. Saying no assertively requires confidence in yourself and your decision-making abilities. Believe in yourself and your ability to make the right choices for your life.

Check Your Body Language. Assertive body language includes maintaining eye contact, standing tall with good posture, and using open gestures. Ensure your body language conveys confidence and assertiveness when interacting with others.

Express Yourself Without Hesitation or Apologies.
Instead of hesitating or apologizing when expressing
your thoughts and feelings, be direct and honest. This
allows you to communicate your needs and wants
effectively and respectfully.

Be Clear in Your Requests. When making requests,
be specific and clear about what you want or need.
This helps to prevent misunderstandings and ensures
that your request is understood and taken seriously.

Acknowledge Other People's Points of View. Being
assertive doesn't mean disregarding other people's
opinions and feelings. Listen to their perspective and
acknowledge their viewpoint, even if you disagree.

Take Small Steps First. Start practicing
assertiveness in low-stakes situations before tackling
more significant issues. This will help you build
confidence and become more comfortable with
assertive behavior.

Overcoming people-pleasing and learning to
say no assertively is a process that takes time and
practice. But with the right mindset and tools, you can
set healthy boundaries and live a more fulfilled life.
Remember, saying no isn't selfish or rude; it's an act
of self-care and self-respect.

Up Next: Boundaries

Removing toxic people from your life and practicing
assertiveness are perfect ways to show yourself that
you love yourself enough not to put up with anything
that negatively impacts your life. This is not to say that
toxic people aren't hovering around the corner,
waiting to do their damage. Boundaries are the only
thing that will stop people that you meet from walking
all over you.

CHAPTER 6
PROTECTING YOURSELF WITH ESSENTIAL BOUNDARIES

*"The only people who get upset about you setting boundaries are
the ones who are benefiting from you having none."*
-Unknown

Healthy boundaries play a crucial role in practicing self-love. By setting boundaries, we can protect ourselves from toxic relationships and create a safe space for personal growth. In this chapter, we will explore the importance of boundaries, the different types of boundaries, and how to set, communicate, and enforce them effectively.

Boundaries are the limits we set for ourselves in terms of how we allow others to treat us, what we will tolerate, and how we will communicate our needs and desires. When we have healthy boundaries, we are able to protect our physical, emotional, and mental well-being. This ultimately leads to a greater sense of self-respect, self-esteem, and self-love.

The Importance of Boundaries

When we set boundaries, we are able to prioritize our own needs and desires. This means that we are not constantly putting other people's needs before our own or sacrificing our own happiness for the sake of others. By prioritizing ourselves, we are sending a message to the world that we value ourselves and our well-being.

Protecting our personal space.

By setting physical and emotional boundaries, we can maintain a sense of privacy and control over our own live and they protect us from being taken advantage of. We know our limits and communicate them clearly, which makes it harder for others to manipulate or coerce us into doing things we don't want to do. When we have healthy boundaries, we are more likely to attract people who respect and value us. We are able to establish relationships that are based on mutual respect and understanding rather than coercion or manipulation.

Preserving Self-Care

Boundaries help us maintain a sense of self-worth and ensure that our needs and feelings are respected by others. And perhaps most importantly, healthy and strong boundaries allow us to prioritize self-care and take time for ourselves without feeling guilty or selfish. We know that taking care of ourselves is essential for our well-being and that setting boundaries is necessary to ensure that we have the time and space we need to rest and recharge. By setting healthy boundaries, we are sending a message to the world that we value ourselves and our well-being, which ultimately leads to a greater sense of self-respect, self-esteem, and self-love.

Preventing Emotional Exhaustion

By establishing limits on how much emotional energy we invest in others, we can prevent burnout and maintain our emotional well-being. When you have healthy boundaries, you reduce the stress and anxiety that comes from feeling overwhelmed or overcommitted.

Promoting Healthy Relationships

Boundaries create a foundation for trust, respect, and open communication in our relationships with others. When you communicate your needs and expectations clearly, others are more likely to respect them. This leads to more fulfilling and supportive relationships.

Discovering Your Boundaries

As discussed in Chapter 4, emotional intelligence is a great place to start for most situations. And figuring out what your boundaries actually are is no different! By listening to what your emotions are telling you, you can discover what your limits are. For example, anger is often a sign of boundaries being crossed. Also, pay attention to your thoughts, especially around particular people. To understand your boundaries, you need to have a clear idea of what types of boundaries exist, and what your values are for each type.

Types of Boundaries

There are several types of boundaries that we can establish to protect ourselves and maintain healthy relationships. Keep a journal of your emotional responses when these types of boundaries come up in your relationships, how they are met or crossed, and how you felt and responded in those moments. Through this practice you'll start to get an idea of areas you can work on, areas you're already comfortable with, and who regularly respects (or disrespects) your boundaries.

Physical boundaries. These refer to our personal space and physical touch. Examples include setting limits on how close someone can stand to us or what kind of physical touch is acceptable.

Emotional boundaries: These pertain to our feelings and emotions. Examples include not taking on other people's emotions as our own or not allowing others to invalidate our feelings.

Mental boundaries. These involve our thoughts, beliefs, and opinions. Examples include not letting others impose their beliefs on us or not feeling obligated to agree with someone else's opinion.

Time boundaries. These relate to how we allocate our time and energy. Examples include setting aside time for self-care, establishing a work-life balance, and not allowing others to infringe on our personal time.

Communication boundaries. These entail the way we communicate with others. Examples include setting limits on the topics we are willing to discuss, avoiding gossip, and not tolerating abusive language.

Setting Boundaries

Setting strong boundaries is an important skill that can help you maintain healthy relationships, avoid burnout, and protect your mental and emotional well-being. However, it can be a challenging task, especially if you're someone who tends to be accommodating or people-pleasing (see Chapter 5 on ways to address being a people pleaser). Lucky for all of us, there are practical and kind ways we can set strong boundaries that are assertive, respectful, and effective. In this answer, I'll share some tips and strategies that can help you set strong boundaries in a way that's assertive, respectful, and effective.

Know Your Limits

The first step in setting strong boundaries is to know your own limits. This means being aware of your physical, emotional, and mental capacities and recognizing when you're feeling overwhelmed, stressed, or burnt out. Once you know your limits, you can start to set boundaries that protect your well-being and prevent you from taking on too much.

Be Clear and Specific

When setting boundaries, it's essential to be clear and specific about what you're comfortable with and what you're not. This means using clear language and avoiding vague or ambiguous statements. For example, instead of saying "I don't like it when you interrupt me," you could say "It's important to me that we take turns speaking during our conversations."

Communicate Assertively

Setting boundaries requires assertive communication skills. This means expressing your needs and preferences in a clear, direct, and respectful manner. It also involves using "I" statements instead of "you" statements to avoid sounding accusatory or confrontational. For example, instead of saying "You're always interrupting me," you could say "I feel frustrated when I'm interrupted during our conversations."

Be Consistent

Consistency is key when it comes to setting strong boundaries. This means enforcing your boundaries consistently, even when it's difficult or uncomfortable. It also means being prepared to say "no" or push back when someone tries to cross your boundaries. By being consistent, you'll send a clear message that your boundaries are non-negotiable and that you're serious about protecting your well-being.

Addressing Boundary Violations

Setting strong boundaries is an essential skill that can help you maintain healthy relationships and protect your well-being. By knowing your limits, being clear and specific, communicating assertively, and being consistent, you can set boundaries that are effective, respectful, and empowering. Remember that setting boundaries is a process, and it takes time and practice to get it right. With patience and perseverance, however, you can become a master of boundary-setting and enjoy healthier, happier relationships as a result.

As a highly skilled assistant, Hannah was used to setting boundaries and having them respected by her clients. But when it came to her best friend, Emily, it was a different story. Emily constantly crossed the line, whether it was canceling plans last minute or showing up uninvited to Hannah's home.

At first, Hannah tried to brush it off. She didn't want to ruin their friendship over what she thought were small things. But the disrespect continued and Hannah found herself feeling more and more frustrated.

One day, she decided enough was enough. She called Emily and asked to meet up for a coffee. Over their drinks, Hannah calmly explained how she felt when Emily didn't respect her boundaries. Emily was taken aback at first, but then apologized and promised to do better.

However, Hannah knew that it would take more than just one conversation to make a lasting change. She continued to communicate her boundaries to Emily and remind her when they were being crossed.

It wasn't always easy, but Hannah knew that her self-respect and mental health were worth it.

Months later, Hannah and Emily's friendship was stronger than ever. Emily had learned to respect Hannah's boundaries and even adopted some for herself. Hannah felt proud of herself for standing up for what she needed, knowing that it had led to a healthier and happier friendship.

As she reflected on the experience, Hannah couldn't help but feel encouraged. She realized that setting boundaries was not only important for her personal and professional life, but also for her relationships. And with each successful boundary she set, she felt both empowered and grateful for the people in her life who respected her enough to honor them.

In some cases, we aren't as lucky to have a friend like Emily, and setting boundaries may not be enough to protect ourselves from toxic relationships. Recognizing and moving on from toxic people is essential for our well-being, and recognizing that violated boundaries are a reflection of the lack of respect our friends, family, colleagues, or bosses have for us should be enough to encourage us to cut ties without guilt.

Knowing When to Cut Ties

Accept the situation. Acknowledge that some people may not respect your boundaries and accept that you may need to distance yourself from them.

Seek support. Reach out to friends, family, or a therapist for guidance and support in dealing with toxic relationships.

Focus on self-care. Prioritize your own well-being and invest time and energy in activities that bring you joy and peace.

Establish new boundaries. Use the experience as an opportunity to reevaluate and strengthen your boundaries to prevent future toxic relationships.

Setting and maintaining boundaries is essential for protecting our emotional, physical, and mental well-being, as well as fostering healthy relationships. By understanding the different types of boundaries, effectively communicating them, and addressing boundary violations, we can create a safe space for personal growth and meaningful connections. Additionally, recognizing and moving on from toxic relationships is crucial for maintaining our overall well-being and happiness.

Up next: Self-Care

For the modern woman, time is certainly limited, and more so if you have children. Having strong, healthy boundaries in place is necessary to ensure you have time for yourself. Without this time, you won't be able to practice self-care.

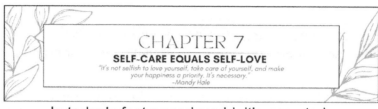

In today's fast-paced world, it's easy to become overwhelmed by the demands of daily life. From juggling work, relationships, and personal goals, it can be challenging to find time for self-care. However, taking care of our physical, emotional, and mental well-being is crucial for cultivating self-love and living a fulfilling life. In this chapter, we will explore what self-care is and why it's essential for self-love. We will also provide practical tips for incorporating self-care into your daily routine, covering various areas such as physical health, emotional wellbeing, mindfulness, empathy, and more.

What is Self-Care?

Self-care is the practice of taking intentional actions to nurture and maintain our overall well-being. It involves engaging in activities that promote physical, emotional, and mental health, allowing us to function at our best and enjoy life to the fullest. Self-care is not a one-size-fits-all concept; it varies person-to-person and evolves as our needs and circumstances change.

Why Self-Care is Crucial for Self-Love

Self-care is the foundation of self-love. It is a powerful way to demonstrate our commitment to ourselves and our well-being. By prioritizing self-care, we acknowledge our worth and value, fostering a healthy sense of self-esteem and self-compassion. Furthermore, self-care allows us to show up as our best selves in all aspects of life, including our relationships, work, and personal growth. We can best see the importance and widespread impact of a strong self-care routine through a story about two women: one with a good self-care routine, and the other with a poor self-care routine.

The first woman took care of herself religiously. She woke up early, went for a run, and ate a healthy breakfast. She made sure to moisturize her skin, brush her teeth twice a day, and get enough sleep. She believed in self-love and made it a priority to take care of herself. She felt that taking care of herself in the big and small ways every day was a way to her love herself.

The second woman, on the other hand, had a different approach to life. She would often skip meals, stay up late, and never found the time to exercise. She rarely washed her face or brushed her teeth, and her hair was always unkempt. She didn't think much of self-care, and her self-love suffered as a result.

One day, the two women met and struck up a conversation. They talked about their lives and their experiences. The woman with the good self-care routine shared how it made her feel confident and happy. She loved the way her body felt after a good workout, and how it helped her stay energized throughout the day. She told the other woman how these small acts of self-care had transformed her life.

The woman with the poor self-care routine was intrigued. She had never thought of taking care of herself in this way. She often started diets only to quit them or promised herself she'd get to the gym every day, only to be discouraged after missing a day here or there. She quit most things because she felt like a failure, and eventually stopped trying. She asked the other woman how she got started and what advice she had for someone like her.

The woman with the good self-care routine encouraged her to start small. She advised her to set achievable goals and to track her progress. When she failed on a day, forgive herself and start again. She told her that self-care was an act of self-love and that it was the key to a happy and healthy life. She explained that she reframed her thought process about everyday tasks to reflect the love they created for her. Small actions like washing her face and going through a 10-step skin routine felt crazy at first, given how busy she was. But when she stopped to thing about how she deserved the time to take care of her skin and ensure she had what she needed before caring for anyone else, everything changed.

The two women parted ways, and the woman with the poor self-care routine decided to take the advice of her new friend. She started with small changes, such as taking a daily walk and drinking more water. She began to feel better and more confident, and her self-love improved.

Emotional Intelligence and Self-Care

Developing emotional intelligence is a vital aspect of self-care, as it enables us to understand, manage, and express our emotions effectively. Cultivating emotional intelligence can lead to improved mental health, better relationships, and increased self-awareness. Here are some strategies for enhancing emotional intelligence:

Practice Self-Awareness

Self-awareness involves recognizing and understanding our emotions, thoughts, and behaviors.

To develop self-awareness, take time to reflect on your emotions and consider their causes and implications. Journaling, meditation, and mindfulness practices can help to promote self-awareness.

Cultivate Empathy

Empathy is the ability to understand and share the feelings of others. To develop empathy, practice active listening, be non-judgmental, and try to see situations from others' perspectives. Cultivating empathy can lead to stronger, more meaningful relationships and a greater sense of connection with others.

Learn Emotional Regulation Techniques

Emotional regulation refers to the process of managing emotions in a healthy and constructive way. It involves recognizing, understanding, and managing one's emotions to reduce the negative impact they may have on oneself and others.

Emotional regulation is an important skill that helps individuals maintain positive relationships, cope with stress, and achieve personal goals. It involves being aware of one's own emotions, identifying triggers, and developing strategies to manage them effectively.

For example, if someone experiences anger or frustration at work, they may use various techniques to regulate their emotions. These techniques may include taking a break, deep breathing exercises, or talking to a trusted friend or colleague.

There are several benefits associated with emotional regulation. One key benefit is that it helps individuals manage stress more effectively. When someone is able to regulate their emotions, they can think more clearly and make better decisions in difficult situations.

Another benefit is that emotional regulation can improve relationships. When someone is able to manage their emotions in a healthy way, they are likely to communicate more effectively and respond to others in a more positive manner.

Emotional regulation is also important for mental health. When someone struggles with emotional regulation, they may experience symptoms of anxiety or depression. Developing healthy emotional regulation skills can help individuals manage these symptoms and improve their overall mental well-being.

There are several strategies that individuals can use to develop their emotional regulation skills. These include mindfulness meditation, cognitive-behavioral therapy, and journaling. It's important to note that everyone's approach to emotional regulation will be unique and what works for one person may not work for another.

Emotional regulation is a critical skill for maintaining positive relationships, managing stress, and achieving personal goals. By developing healthy emotional regulation strategies, individuals can improve their mental well-being and lead happier, more fulfilling lives.

Mindfulness and Self-Care

Mindfulness is the practice of paying attention to our thoughts, emotions, and bodily sensations in the present moment without judgment. Incorporating mindfulness into our self-care routine can lead to improved mental well-being, reduced stress, and increased self-awareness. We'll discuss mindfulness practices in greater detail in Chapter 11, but below are some tips for getting started.

Engage in Meditation

Meditation is a powerful tool for cultivating mindfulness and enhancing mental well-being. Regular meditation practice can help to alleviate stress, improve focus, and promote emotional stability. Start with short sessions of 5-10 minutes per day and gradually increase the duration as you become more comfortable with the practice.

Practice Mindful Breathing

Mindful breathing involves focusing on the sensation of your breath as it moves in and out of your body. To practice mindful breathing, find a comfortable sitting position, close your eyes, and bring your attention to your breath. Observe each inhalation and exhalation without judgment, and gently bring your focus back to your breath if your mind wanders.

Incorporate Mindfulness into Daily Activities

You can incorporate mindfulness into everyday activities by paying attention to your senses and being fully present in the moment. For example, practice mindful eating by savoring the flavors, textures, and aromas of your food, or engage in mindful walking by focusing on the sensation of your feet touching the ground.

Empathy and Self-Care

Empathy is a powerful tool that can greatly impact our lives in a multitude of ways. When we talk about empathy in the context of self-care, it refers to the ability to understand and share the feelings of others, as well as to be able to recognize and manage our own emotions. So how is empathy important for self-care? Let's take a closer look.

It helps us connect with others. Empathy is all about understanding and sharing the feelings of others. By developing this skill, we can better connect with those around us, which can be incredibly beneficial for our mental and emotional well-being. When we feel connected to others, we're more likely to feel supported, understood, and loved, which can help us cope with stress, anxiety, and other challenges.

It helps us regulate our own emotions. In addition to understanding the feelings of others, empathy also involves being able to recognize and regulate our own emotions. When we're able to do this, we're better equipped to manage stress, anxiety, and other negative emotions that can take a toll on our mental and physical health. By practicing empathy, we can learn to be more compassionate with ourselves and others, which can help us feel more grounded and at peace.

It promotes a sense of community. Empathy is a key component of building strong relationships and creating a sense of community. When we're able to understand and share the feelings of others, we're more likely to work together towards common goals and support each other through difficult times. This sense of community can be incredibly powerful for our mental and emotional well-being, as it can provide us with a sense of belonging and purpose.

It helps us make better decisions. When we're able to empathize with others, we're more likely to make decisions that are compassionate and understanding. This can be incredibly important when it comes to self-care, as it can help us make choices that prioritize our own well-being as well as the well-being of those around us. By practicing empathy, we can become more attuned to the needs and feelings of ourselves and others, which can help us make better decisions in all areas of our lives.

Empathy is an incredibly important skill when it comes to self-care. By developing this skill, we can better connect with others, regulate our own emotions, promote a sense of community, and make better decisions. So if you're looking to improve your self-care routine, consider practicing empathy as a way to enhance your mental and emotional well-being.

Making Self-Care a Daily Practice

Create a Self-Care Plan. Develop a personalized self-care plan that includes activities and practices that nourish your physical, emotional, and mental well-being. Identify specific self-care goals and schedule time each day to engage in these activities.

Set Boundaries. Establishing healthy boundaries is essential for maintaining self-love and prioritizing self-care. Communicate your needs and limits to others, and practice saying "no" when necessary to protect your well-being.

Seek Support. Connecting with supportive friends, family members, or a therapist can help you stay accountable to your self-care goals and provide encouragement along the way.

Moving Forward

Self-care is an essential aspect of self-love, as it allows us to prioritize our well-being and cultivate a strong sense of self-worth. By incorporating self-care practices that address our physical, emotional, and mental health, we can lead more fulfilling, balanced lives. Remember, self-care is a lifelong journey, and it's never too late to start prioritizing your well-being.

Up next: Stress

The great thing about self-care is that it gives you the energy to handle the endless responsibilities you have and the challenges that come your way. It's much easier to resolve a problem when you have had a good night's sleep. One thing that can throw your self-care routine off is stress!

Stress is an inevitable part of life. Everyone experiences it at some point, and some people experience it more frequently than others. While it can motivate us to get things done, it can also become a source of overwhelming anxiety and poor health when left unmanaged.

Learning how to manage stress effectively is crucial to maintain a balanced lifestyle and overall well-being. By learning how to manage your stress, you will become stronger and more resilient, ultimately improving your overall quality of life and ability to continue your journey toward self-love and acceptance.

Understanding Stress and Its Impact on Your Life

Stress is the body's natural response to a perceived threat or challenge. Just like every living creature on earth, our biology has built-in triggers to help keep us safe. When you encounter a situation that your brain perceives as dangerous or stressful, it triggers the release of hormones such as cortisol and adrenaline. These hormones prepare your body for the "fight, flight, or freeze" response, which can help you respond to the stressful situation quickly.

While stress is a natural response, prolonged exposure to it can negatively affect your physical and mental health. Chronic stress can lead to various health problems, including high blood pressure, heart disease, depression, and anxiety. It can even be the root cause of digestive problems, poor sleep quality, and nightmares and affect your relationships, work performance, and overall quality of life. By understanding the potential dangers and symptoms of stress, we can better recognize when it's essential to manage and reduce our stress levels.

Symptoms of Stress

Stress manifests differently for everyone, but there are some common symptoms to look out for. When we're feeling exhausted, ill, or simply feeling moody, it's normal to treat the symptom, without realizing that the root cause is what actually needs attention. It's important to recognize how far and wide the impacts of stress can have on our bodies and minds. So, how do you know when you're too stressed?

Do any of these apply to you? They might be stress-related!

You're constantly tired. Feeling exhausted all the time, even after a good night's sleep, can be a sign of too much stress. Stress can cause sleep disturbances and make it difficult for you to get the rest you need.

You're forgetful. Stress can affect your ability to concentrate and remember things. If you find yourself forgetting important dates or appointments, it could be a sign that your stress levels are too high.

You're easily irritated. When you're under a lot of stress, it can make you more irritable and short-tempered than usual. You may find yourself snapping at people or getting upset over minor things.

You're experiencing physical symptoms. Stress can manifest in a variety of physical symptoms such as headaches, muscle tension, stomach problems, and chest pain. If you're experiencing any of these symptoms regularly, it's important to talk to your doctor.

You're not enjoying things you used to. If you find that activities that used to bring you joy no longer do, it could be a sign that your stress levels are too high. Stress can rob you of the ability to enjoy life and make it difficult to find pleasure in anything.

You're not taking care of yourself. When you're too stressed, it can be easy to neglect self-care. This can include things like not eating properly, not exercising, or not taking time for yourself. If you find that you're not taking care of yourself as well as you should be, it could be a sign that your stress levels are too high.

If you're experiencing any of these signs, it's important to take steps to manage your stress levels. This can include things like practicing relaxation techniques, getting regular exercise, talking to a therapist, or making lifestyle changes to reduce stress. Remember, managing stress is an important part of maintaining your overall health and well-being.

Recognizing the many possible symptoms of stress in yourself or a loved one can be the first step in addressing and managing stress levels, and the benefits of proper stress management are huge! From increased energy and focus levels, better sleep quality, and a stronger immune system to improved work performance and overall mental health, your body and mind can't afford to take stress levels for granted.

Common Causes of Stress

Stress can come from a variety of sources, and different people may experience stress differently. It's important to continue the self-reflection practices we discussed in Chapter 1 to stay on top of how you're feeling, what you're struggling with, and what is working (and not working) for you in your life.

The first step in managing stress is identifying the situations or events that trigger your stress response. This can help you anticipate and prepare for stressful situations and avoid unnecessary stress. Try keeping a stress journal for a week or two to identify your stress triggers. Write down the situations or events that cause you stress and your thoughts, feelings, and physical sensations.

Examples of Common Stressors

Work-Related. Deadlines, workload, or interpersonal conflicts on the job.

Financial. Debt, job loss, or unexpected expenses.

Relational. Relationship stress, such as conflicts with your partner, family, or friends. Toxic relationships, as discussed in Chapter 5, can be especially stressful.

Medical. Health-related stress, such as chronic illness, injury, or disability.

Big Changes. Life transitions, such as getting married, having a baby, or moving to a new city.

Then, once you have identified your stress triggers, you can start to develop coping strategies to manage them. Just make sure you don't wait too long! A good friend of mine, Abby, constantly struggles with her stress levels, but will never again let herself reach the point she did last summer.

Abby had always been a hard worker, pushing herself to the limits to climb the corporate ladder. But lately, she had been feeling the weight of the world on her shoulders. The endless meetings, the never-ending emails, and the constant pressure to perform were all starting to take their toll on her.

She tried to keep up with everything, hoping that things would eventually get better. But they didn't. The stress kept piling up, and she found herself struggling to cope. She would come home exhausted and drained, unable to do much more than collapse onto the couch and stare blankly at the television.

Her friends and family started to notice the change in her. She was always irritable and short-tempered, and even the simplest things would set her off. Her husband tried to talk to her about it, but she brushed him off, telling him that she was fine and that she just needed to work harder.

But deep down, she knew that something was wrong. She couldn't keep going like this. She needed to take a break, to step back and reassess her priorities. And yet, she couldn't bring herself to do it. The thought of taking time off work filled her with anxiety and guilt.

It wasn't until she finally hit rock bottom that she realized just how much she had been letting work stress take over her life. She found herself sobbing uncontrollably in her car one day, unable to even summon the energy to get out and go to work. It was then that she knew that something had to change.

And so she quit her job, without a backup plan or any clear idea of what she would do next. It was a terrifying decision, but also a liberating one. For the first time in years, she felt like she had a choice in her own life. And as she walked out of her office for the last time, she knew that this was just the beginning of a new journey.

Practical Tips for Managing Stress

Now that we understand the dangers of stress and its symptoms, let's explore some techniques to help manage and prevent stress from taking over our lives. Just like how we all experience stress in different ways, we also each have different practices that will help us on our personal journey. Take a look at common ways to manage your stress below, and give each a try to see what works best for you.

Prioritize Self-Care. Self-care is essential for managing stress and maintaining good health and well-being. When you prioritize self-care, you can better cope with stress and prevent burnout. Make time for activities that you enjoy and that help you relax, such as reading, taking a bath, or listening to music. Continue the practices that work best for you as we discussed in Chapter 7.

Practice Mindfulness. Mindfulness is a powerful tool for managing stress and improving your overall well-being. We discussed practices similar to these in prior chapters, but we'll dig even deeper into them in our last chapter. Mindfulness is being present and "in the moment", and focusing on your thoughts and feelings without judgment. You can practice mindfulness by meditating, doing yoga, or simply taking a few minutes to focus on your breathing.

Common Mindfulness Techniques

- Mindful breathing: Take a few minutes to focus on your breath, inhaling and exhaling slowly and deeply.

- Body scan: Lie down or sit comfortably and focus on each part of your body, noticing any sensations or feelings without judgment.

- Mindful eating: Take time to savor your food, paying attention to the taste, texture, and aroma.

- Mindful walking: Take a walk and focus on your surroundings, noticing the sights, sounds, and smells.

Get Regular Exercise

Exercise is a natural stress reliever and can help improve your mood and mental health. When you exercise, your body releases feel-good chemicals called endorphins, which can help reduce stress and anxiety. Regular exercise can also help you sleep better and improve your physical health. Aim for at least 30 minutes of moderate daily exercise, such as jogging, cycling, or swimming. Don't forget that this isn't a one-size-fits-all routine, either! As discussed in Chapter 7, find what practice works best for you.

Eat a Healthy Diet

A healthy diet can help support your mental and physical health and can also help you manage stress. Eating a balanced diet that includes plenty of fruits, vegetables, whole grains, and lean protein can help reduce inflammation in the body and support healthy brain function. Avoiding processed foods, sugar, and caffeine can also help reduce stress and anxiety. Speak with your doctor about a personal diet that works for you and any potential vitamin regimes you could benefit from.

Get Enough Sleep

Sleep is essential for good health and well-being and can also help you manage stress. Most healthcare providers recommend 7-9 hours of sleep per night, and getting too little (or too much!) can lead to more stress.

Ask the Professionals

If you are experiencing chronic stress or struggling to manage it on your own, it may be helpful to seek professional help. A therapist or counselor can provide you with tools and strategies for managing stress and help you explore the underlying causes of your stress. In some cases, medication may also help manage stress and anxiety. You don't have to go through the struggle alone!

Trained professionals can provide you with the tools and techniques you need to manage your stress and build resilience. They can also help you identify the underlying causes of your stress and develop a plan for addressing them.

Another way that professionals can help you manage stress is by teaching you relaxation techniques such as deep breathing, meditation, or yoga. These techniques have been proven to be effective in reducing stress levels and improving overall well-being. They can also be practiced anywhere and at any time, making them ideal for busy professionals who may not have a lot of free time.

In addition to counseling and relaxation techniques, professionals can also help you develop healthy habits that can reduce your stress levels over time. This might include regular exercise, a healthy diet, and getting enough sleep each night. By taking care of your physical health, you can build up your resilience to stress and improve your overall quality of life.

Finally, professionals can also help you create a more balanced work-life schedule that prioritizes self-care and leisure time. This might involve setting boundaries with work emails and phone calls outside of office hours, taking regular breaks throughout the day, and setting aside time each week for hobbies or other activities that bring you joy.

Managing stress is an important part of maintaining a healthy work-life balance, and professionals can play a key role in helping you achieve this goal. Whether through counseling, relaxation techniques, healthy habits, or lifestyle changes, working with a professional can give you the tools and support you need to reduce your stress levels and improve your overall well-being.

Stress is a normal and natural part of life, but it can become harmful if not managed properly. By understanding the impact of stress on your life, identifying your stress triggers, and practicing stress management techniques such as self-care, mindfulness, exercise, and a healthy diet, you can take control of your life and improve your overall well-being.

Remember that managing stress is a lifelong process, and asking for help when needed is okay. We're all in this together.

Up Next: Self-Esteem & Self-Worth

Managing stress is crucial for your physical well-being as much as it is for your mental health. It gives the mind a chance to calm down, even some breathing space to think about the bigger things in life...like how much you are worth!

Embracing a healthy sense of self-esteem and self-worth is essential for overall well-being and personal fulfillment. These two interconnected concepts play a vital role in how we perceive ourselves and the world around us. Self-esteem and self-worth are two terms that are often used interchangeably, but they actually have different meanings. Understanding the difference between the two can help you better understand how to cultivate a healthy sense of self, ultimately helping you to unlock your full potential and lead a more satisfying, confident life.

Understanding Self-Esteem and Self-Worth

What is Self-Esteem?

Self-esteem is a term used to describe the degree to which you value yourself as a person and how much you think others value you. It is influenced by various factors, such as our upbringing, experiences, and personal achievements. A healthy level of self-esteem enables us to accept and appreciate ourselves, fostering resilience and a positive outlook on life. When we have high self-esteem, we tend to be more confident, resilient, and assertive. We're able to handle challenges and setbacks better, and we're more likely to pursue our goals. On the other hand, when we have low self-esteem, we tend to doubt ourselves, be more anxious, and avoid taking risks.

What is Self-Worth?

Self-worth, on the other hand, refers to your intrinsic value as a person, regardless of what you do or what others think of you. It is the recognition that we are deserving of love, respect, and dignity, regardless of our achievements, failures, or external circumstances. Developing a strong sense of self-worth allows us to cultivate self-compassion and self-acceptance, empowering us to face life's challenges with confidence and grace.

It's important to note that self-esteem and self-worth can both impact our mental health and well-being. People with high self-esteem may feel confident and capable, but if their self-esteem is based solely on external factors, they may struggle with feelings of insecurity and inadequacy when faced with failure or rejection. Alternatively, those with high self-worth may be more resilient in the face of adversity because they have an unshakeable sense of their own value as a person.

Simply put, self-esteem is about how we perceive ourselves in relation to others, while self-worth is about recognizing our inherent value as individuals. Both are important for our mental health and well-being and cultivating a healthy sense of both can help us lead happier and more fulfilling lives.

Causes of Low Self-Esteem and Low Self-Worth

Both low self-worth and low self-esteem stem from a combination of external and internal factors, often debated within a nature vs. nurture context - how much of our personality comes from our DNA, and how much of it comes from our experiences? It's generally accepted that genetics and biology contribute to approximately 50% of an individual's self-esteem and self-worth, encompassing personality traits, predispositions, and psychological makeup. The remaining 50% is shaped by life experiences, with early childhood experiences playing a crucial role. Parenting strategies, in particular, can have a substantial impact, with highly critical, abusive, or neglectful parents causing the most damage. Later in life, severe trauma or abusive relationships can also contribute to low self-esteem or low self-worth.

Recognizing the Signs of Low Self-Worth and Low Self-Esteem

Low self-esteem and self-worth can manifest in various ways, affecting your thoughts, feelings, and behaviors. One of my readers submitted this story, which directly highlights how important self-esteem and self-worth are.

"I never thought I'd be able to write this story. But here I am, on the other side of my pain, sharing my journey of self-discovery and worth. It all started when I was just a kid, growing up in a chaotic household. My parents divorced when I was eight, and my life was turned upside down. My mom struggled with addiction and depression, and my dad was always working, trying to provide for us.

I was left feeling alone, unloved, and unworthy of anything good. As I grew older, my self-esteem plummeted. I found myself in toxic relationships, trying to gain validation and love from others. I turned to drugs and alcohol to numb the pain, but that only made things worse.

It wasn't until I hit rock bottom that I realized something had to change. I couldn't keep living my life this way. So I made the decision to get help and started counseling. It was a tough journey, but slowly and surely, I started to gain some self-worth.

My therapist taught me that I am not my past, and I don't have to let it define me. I learned to forgive myself and others for the pain I had experienced. I started to focus on self-love and positive affirmations, repeating them every day until they became a part of me.

It wasn't easy, but I surrounded myself with positive and supportive people who believed in me. And slowly but surely, I started to see changes in myself. I started to believe that I was worthy of love and happiness, and I began to attract more positive experiences into my life.

Now, as I sit here writing this story, I'm amazed at how far I've come. I never thought I'd be able to overcome my childhood trauma, but I did. I learned that self-worth isn't something that can be given to you by others, it's something that you have to find within yourself.

And as I look to the future, I know that my journey isn't over yet. But I'm excited to see where it takes me, knowing that I have the strength and self-worth to face anything that comes my way."

When you're in the midst of struggling, it can be overwhelming and difficult to recognize that something is going on internally. This is yet another powerful reason keeping a journal and being in touch with your feelings, emotions, and inner thoughts can be a powerful tool against falling into the depths of these behaviors. Have you experienced any of these feelings or behaviors?

- Difficulty focusing and functioning in work, school, or other important tasks.

- Negative changes in mood, such as increased stress, anxiety, irritability, or sadness.

- Neglecting or procrastinating essential tasks at work, school, or home.

- Inconsistency in self-care, exercise, and wellness routines.

- Negative self-talk, pessimism, and self-criticism.

- Self-doubt and difficulty setting goals, making decisions, and taking on challenges.

- Social isolation, withdrawal, or lashing out towards others.

- Overusing unhealthy outlets, such as drugs, alcohol, or social media distractions.

- Poor boundary-setting or allowing others to disrespect or mistreat you.

Assessing Your Self-Worth: The Self-Worth Scale

Rosenberg's self-esteem scale is a popular and widely used psychological tool that measures an individual's level of self-esteem. It consists of 10 statements that measure an individual's self-worth, self-acceptance, and overall feelings of self-confidence.

The statements in the scale include statements like "I feel that I am a person of worth, at least on an equal plane with others," "I feel that I am a failure," and "On the whole, I am satisfied with myself." Participants are asked to rate how strongly they agree or disagree with each statement on a scale from 1 to 4, with 1 being strongly disagree and 4 being strongly agree.

The scale was developed by Morris Rosenberg, a sociologist who wanted to create a reliable and valid measure of self-esteem that could be used in research studies. Since its development in the 1960s, the Rosenberg self-esteem scale has become one of the most widely used measures of self-esteem in psychology.

So why is Rosenberg's self-esteem scale useful? Well, for starters, it is a quick and easy way to measure an individual's level of self-esteem. This makes it useful for researchers who are studying self-esteem in various populations, as well as for clinicians who are working with individuals who may have low self-esteem.

In addition, the scale has been found to be reliable and valid across a variety of different populations, including adolescents, adults, and individuals from different cultural backgrounds. This means that the scale can be used with confidence in a wide range of settings.

Rosenberg self-esteem scale has been shown to be a good predictor of various outcomes related to mental health and well-being. For example, individuals with low self-esteem are more likely to experience depression, anxiety, and other mental health issues. By measuring an individual's level of self-esteem using this scale, researchers and clinicians can identify individuals who may be at risk for these issues and provide appropriate interventions.

In summary, Rosenberg's self-esteem scale is a valuable tool for measuring an individual's level of self-esteem. It is quick, easy to administer, and has been shown to be reliable and valid across a variety of different populations. Additionally, the scale can be used to predict various outcomes related to mental health and well-being, making it a useful tool for researchers and clinicians alike.

Rosenburg's Self-Esteem Scale Questionnaire

Answer the 10 questions below with either Strongly Agree, Agree, Disagree, or Strongly Disagree

1. I feel that I am a person of worth, at least on an equal plane with others.
2. I feel that I have a number of good qualities.
3. All in all, I am inclined to feel that I am a failure.
4. I am able to do things as well as most other people.
5. I feel I do not have much to be proud of.
6. I take a positive attitude toward myself.
7. On the whole, I am satisfied with myself.
8. I wish I could have more respect for myself.
9. I certainly feel useless at times.
10. At times, I think I am no good at all.

Scoring Your Self-Esteem Questionnaire

Next, tally up your scores based on the following calculations. Make sure you pay close attention to the scores you provided based on each question, because they are different!

For questions 1, 2, 4, 6, and 7, give yourself 3 points for anytime you answered "Strongly Agree", 2 points for anytime you answered "Agree", 1 point for anytime you answered "Disagree", and 0 points for anytime you answered "Strongly Disagree".

For questions 3, 5, 8, 9, and 10, give yourself 0 points for anytime you answered "Strongly Agree", 1 point for anytime you answered "Agree", 2 points for anytime you answered "Disagree", and 3 points for anytime you answered "Strongly Disagree".

Understanding Your Self-Esteem Score

Once you've tallied up your score above, you should have a number between 0 and 30. Scores between 15 and 25 are within the "Normal" range for self-esteem, scores between 26-30 are considered high in self-esteem, and scores below 15 are considered low on the self-esteem scale.

Reflecting on Your Self-Esteem Score

Was your score what you generally expected to see? Was it higher or lower than you thought it would be? This is a simple way to get a baseline of where you're at personally, but by no means should it be taken as 100% fact. Simple use this as a starting point for self-reflection on how you feel about yourself and where to go from here. Moving forward let's talk about ways to boot your self-esteem and self-worth.

Strategies for Boosting Self-Esteem and Self-Worth

If you or a loved one is struggling with low self-esteem or self-worth, you're not alone! These impact many of us on a daily basis, and the work we put in today will pay dividends tomorrow when it comes to high self-esteem, self-worth, and self-love. And the good news is that there are many tried and true ways to work on increasing our self-esteem and self-worth.

Be kind to yourself. Practicing self-compassion has been proven to offer numerous benefits, including better health, happiness, and success. Be kinder in your self-talk and treat yourself with understanding and forgiveness. Self-compassion also involves treating ourselves with kindness, understanding, and acceptance. We can do this by acknowledging our mistakes and imperfections without judgment, and by being gentle and supportive with ourselves. Refer back to Chapter 2 for ways to forgive ourselves for not being perfect!

Challenge negative self-talk. Remember our discussion about Automatic Negative Thoughts (ANTs) in Chapter 3? That rude voice inside our head isn't real, and it isn't nice. Negative self-talk can be damaging to our self-esteem. We can challenge negative self-talk by questioning its validity, replacing it with positive affirmations, and focusing on our strengths and accomplishments. Cultivating a positive mindset is essential for fostering high self-worth and combating negative thinking patterns. Embrace challenges as opportunities for growth, learn from your mistakes, and focus on your successes rather than your failures.

Stop looking outside yourself for validation. Relying on external sources for approval, such as your boss, social media followers, or friends, can provide a temporary boost to your self-esteem and self-worth, but ultimately traps you in a cycle of dependence. Focus on cultivating an internal sense of validation instead. Interrupt the cycle of comparisons and judgments by focusing on finding common ground and building connections with others. This will help you feel more connected and less focused on measuring your self-worth against others.

Separate what you do from who you are. Basing your self-worth on your job can be detrimental to your mental and emotional well-being. Jobs can change or disappear unexpectedly, leaving you scrambling to rebuild your sense of self. It's essential to separate your worth as a person from your professional achievements and maintain a healthy work-life balance. Avoid defining your identity, worth, or value based on your achievements, failures, or external factors. Focus on connecting with your core values, beliefs, and feelings to develop a deeper understanding of your true self.

Set realistic goals. Setting realistic goals can help us build confidence and self-esteem. We can break down larger goals into smaller, achievable ones, and celebrate our progress along the way. Celebrating small wins can help us stay motivated and focused on our goals. We can do this by acknowledging our progress and accomplishments and by rewarding ourselves for a job well done.

Embracing Your Worth and Unlocking Your Full Potential

Cultivating a healthy sense of self-esteem and self-worth is an ongoing process that requires self-awareness, self-compassion, and a commitment to personal growth. By understanding the importance of these concepts and implementing effective strategies to enhance them, you can unlock your full potential and lead a more confident, fulfilling life. Most importantly, self-esteem and self-worth are essential components to achieving self-love. Remember, you are worthy of love and respect and deserve to live a life reflecting your inherent value. Embrace your worth and go forth with confidence and purpose.

Next up: Empowerment

In practicing self-love, you can appreciate just how much worth you have as a human being. But the journey doesn't end here. The period of time spent without self-love often leads to forgetting about dreams and aspirations. As self-esteem starts to grow, it's time to get back on track to realizing your aspirations.

As women, there's nothing more empowering than recognizing the power within ourselves. We already play a vital role in shaping society economically, socially, and politically, but many of us still feel lost, forgotten, or unfulfilled. It's easy to get bogged down by life's challenges and society's injustices. Still, by cultivating a growth mindset, we can unleash our full potential in personal growth and empowerment for ourselves and each other.

What is a Growth Mindset?

The concept of a growth mindset was first introduced by psychologist Carol Dweck in her book *Mindset: The New Psychology of Success.* A growth mindset is about believing that our abilities and talents can be developed through hard work, dedication, and perseverance. It's the belief that we can learn and improve and that our potential is limitless. Embracing a growth mindset enables women to see opportunities instead of obstacles and to challenge themselves to learn and grow.

A fixed mindset is the belief that our abilities and talents are predetermined and that we can't change them. People with a fixed mindset often shy away from challenges and feedback, seeing it as a reflection of their inherent abilities. They may also feel threatened by the success of others, as it reinforces their belief that their own abilities are limited.

The Importance of Having a Growth Mindset as a Woman

As women, we face unique challenges in our personal and professional lives. We may be told that we're not good enough, that we don't belong in certain spaces, or that we should prioritize others over ourselves. These messages can be discouraging, but we can overcome them by cultivating a growth mindset and achieving our goals.

Having a growth mindset allows us to embrace challenges and view them as opportunities for growth. It helps us to see failure as a temporary setback rather than a reflection of our abilities. It also allows us to learn from feedback and use it to improve ourselves rather than taking it as a personal attack.

Cultivating a Growth Mindset for Personal Growth and Empowerment

Changing our mindset isn't always easy, but it is worthwhile. To cultivate a growth mindset, we must identify and challenge our current beliefs and thought patterns. We must embrace new experiences, learn from mistakes, and seek feedback to improve and grow. Over the course of this book, we've discussed and put into practice many ways to develop self-love. A growth mindset is another powerful tool in your self-love toolbox.

A growth mindset is a belief that you can develop your talents, abilities, and intelligence through hard work, dedication, and perseverance. It's common to hear about growth vs. fixed mindsets in professional settings. Goal setting is also something that workplaces provide lots of training on. However, this is a practice that transcends our work and personal lives and should be applied in every aspect of how we live. This is a powerful way to transform our lives and achieve our goals, and it acts as a bridge towards adopting self-love practices daily.

Mindset Changes: Tips for Getting Started

Embrace challenges. Challenges are growth opportunities. When you face a challenge, instead of feeling discouraged or defeated, see it as an opportunity to learn and improve. Embrace the challenge and focus on what you can do to overcome it.

Learn from failure. Failure is not the opposite of success; it's part of the journey toward success. Don't be afraid of failure; embrace it as a learning opportunity. When you fail, take the time to reflect on what went wrong and what you can do differently next time.

Believe in your potential. Believe that you have the potential to grow and learn. Don't limit yourself by thinking that you're not smart enough or talented enough. Instead, focus on your strengths and work on improving your weaknesses.

Emphasize effort over talent. Instead of focusing on your innate abilities, focus on the effort you put in. When you work hard and put in the effort, you can achieve anything you set your mind to.

Surround yourself with positive influences. Surround yourself with people who have a growth mindset and who believe in your potential. Avoid negative influences who try to bring you down or limit your potential.

Keep learning! Keep learning new things and expanding your knowledge. Read books, take courses, and seek out new experiences that challenge you and help you grow.

By adopting a growth mindset, you can transform your life and achieve your goals. It takes time and effort, but with dedication and perseverance, anything is possible. A close friend, Audrey, loves to tell a story about her experience turning 40 and the challenges of adapting to a growth mindset when it came to expectations she had for her life.

Audrey had always dreaded the thought of turning 40. To her, it was a milestone that represented the end of youthfulness. She often pictured herself as a frail old woman with wrinkles spread across her face and a hunch in her back. But as her 39th birthday approached, she found herself in a different frame of mind. She decided to sit down and make a list of what she wanted to achieve by the time she hit 40. At first, the list was rather empty, filled only with vague aspirations. It wasn't easy to articulate what she truly wanted, but she persisted.

Slowly but surely, she began to fill her list with specific goals. She wanted to travel more, learn a new language, start a business, and volunteer in her community. As she wrote down her goals, she realized that she had never given herself permission to dream big. She either felt she had "plenty of time later" to focus on these non-career-focused goals, or she was too distracted by getting through her day-to-day to even think about them.

With newfound clarity and determination, Audrey began working towards her new goals. She started taking online classes, attending networking events, and volunteering at her local food bank. She even went on a solo trip to Europe, something she had always wanted to do but never found the courage to embark on.

By the time Audrey turned 40, she had accomplished most of her goals. She had a thriving business, spoke fluent French, had traveled to over 10 countries, and had made a positive impact in her community. But more than that, Audrey had cultivated a growth mindset that allowed her to *enjoy the process* of achieving her goals. It may be a cliche, but it's true - half the journey is getting there!

As she blew out her 40 candles, Audrey felt grateful for the opportunities that lay ahead. She realized that age was just a number and that with a growth mindset, anything was possible.

Embracing the Power Within to Become an Empowered Woman

Cultivating a growth mindset is a powerful tool for personal growth and empowerment. By embracing challenges, setting goals, and surrounding ourselves with supportive people, we can unleash our full potential and achieve success beyond our wildest dreams. Remember to be kind to yourself, embrace change, and always believe in your own potential. With a growth mindset, anything is possible.

Up Next: Daily Self-Love Practices

In our final chapter and strategy for self-love, we are going to discover simple self-love practices that build on what we've already learned. These practices don't have to take up a lot of time, but they do act as a long-term practice for the ongoing journey of self-love.

CHAPTER 11

DAILY SELF-LOVE PRACTICES

"Don't forget to tell yourself positive things daily! You must love yourself internally to glow externally."
-Hannah Bronfman

As someone who has struggled with self-love throughout my life, I know firsthand how challenging it can be to prioritize the relationship I have with myself. But over the years, I have come to understand the importance of practicing mindfulness to cultivate a deeper sense of self-love and acceptance. In this last strategy for self-love, I'll review the concepts I've found most impactful in my life. I will explore the idea of self-love and mindfulness and share different techniques and practices that can help you unlock the benefits of a more mindful life, just like they did for me.

Understanding the Concept of Self-Love and Mindfulness

Before we dive into the specifics of practicing mindfulness, it's important to first understand what self-love means. By this point, we've gone through an entire book together about self-love! So, let's make sure we're on the same page. Self-love is the practice of accepting and appreciating yourself for who you are, flaws, and all. It's about treating yourself with the same kindness, compassion, and understanding that you would offer to a good friend.

Mindfulness is the act of being present and fully engaged in the moment without judgment or distraction. It involves bringing your attention to the present moment and noticing and accepting your thoughts and feelings without reacting or getting caught up in them.

When we combine self-love and mindfulness, we can create a powerful tool for personal growth and transformation. By being mindful of our thoughts and feelings, we can become more aware of our patterns and tendencies and shift them in a more positive direction. And by practicing self-love, we can cultivate a deeper sense of acceptance and compassion toward ourselves, which can help us navigate life's challenges with greater ease and grace.

What it Means to Be Mindful

So, what exactly does it mean to be mindful? At its core, mindfulness is about being fully present in the moment and noticing and accepting your thoughts and feelings as they arise. This can be easier said than done, especially if you're someone who tends to get caught up in your thoughts or emotions. As you go through these practices, be easy on yourself. It's normal to let day-to-day details get in the way of your journey. Don't get discouraged when your grocery lists and to-do lists try and distract you from your self-reflection. It gets easier with practice!

In this chapter, we'll dig into tangible ways you can learn to be mindful, both in the physical and metaphysical sense. From grounding exercises and deep breathing to yoga and meditation, these techniques offer multiple ways to cultivate a greater sense of calm and peacefulness and help you become more aware of your thoughts and feelings as they arise. As we've discussed throughout this book, self-love, above all else, requires knowing yourself and reflecting on your body and mind.

The Benefits of Practicing Mindfulness

There are many benefits to practicing mindfulness, including increased self-awareness, improved focus and concentration, and greater emotional stability and resilience. Not to mention, it's the cornerstone of being in tune with your sense of self and genuinely developing self-love. By becoming more aware of our thoughts and feelings, we can begin to identify patterns and tendencies that may be holding us back. Awareness is the first step to consciously work toward shifting these thoughts and feelings in a more positive direction.

One of the key benefits of mindfulness is that it can help us become more present in our daily lives. By focusing our attention on the present moment, we can become more fully engaged in our experiences and can savor the small moments of joy and beauty that might otherwise go unnoticed. This can help us cultivate a greater sense of gratitude and appreciation, which can, in turn, increase feelings of self-love and happiness.

Deep Breathing

It might sound silly, but the foundation of all mindfulness practices center around deep breathing. From grounding practices to meditation and yoga, the way we breathe - and monitor our breathing - plays a vital role in how well we connect with our inner selves. The benefits of these practices rely on our ability to focus our attention on the rhythm and depth of our breath. Before we discuss any other techniques, let's review how to breathe well.

The best part about learning to breathe with intention is that you can do it anywhere. Sure, a crowded subway or busy office probably isn't the most relaxing and distraction-free environment for it, but once you've perfected the exercise, you can employ it anywhere and at any time. And these hectic environments will be exactly where you need them most.

I learned the importance of deep breathing, ironically, in a doctor's office. After a work-related back injury, I spent years in debilitating pain. One of the required treatment methods involved getting semi-regular injections into my spine to help with swelling and numb the pain enough so I could walk. The result of these treatments was invaluable. In fact, my mobility and daily life relied heavily on them. The downside? Despite my deathly fear of even the smallest, thinnest needles, every injection was made with a six-inch epidural shot.

The first time I walked into the office for this treatment, my blood pressure immediately shot up to 146/106. In order to get the shot, I had to keep my blood pressure in a safe zone of 120/80. If you're like me and these numbers mean nothing ot you, suffice it to say, I was not doing a good job staying in the safe zone. My heart rate was through the roof, and my already–weak body was crumbling at the thought of a needle going into my back.

Knowing that these appointments become available only every few months, my doctor (bless her heart) was not going to let me leave without this treatment. She sat me down, explained the blood pressure requirements, and walked me through the Square Breathing Method for controlling my breath and heart rate. Within ten minutes of this practice, I was able to get my blood pressure low enough to get the shot. I still didn't like it, but I received the necessary treatment safely, all with the power of deep breathing.

The Square Breathing Method

By focusing on your breath, you can quiet your mind and become more present. First, simply take a moment to listen to your breath. If you're stressed, you will probably notice it's a bit labored, or maybe you feel like you can't breathe at all. I promise — you can. Focus on the breath, in and out. Pay attention to your body as your breath enters your lungs when you inhale and leaves your body on exhale. Are your shoulders tight? How's your posture? Did you sit up as soon as you read that question? I bet you did.

Brené Brown has an excellent technique I use daily for breathing — a 4-part, square breathing method. When going through this exercise, picture (or draw!) a square. Each of the four sides represents an action you will take in your breathing for four counts each. If sitting, make sure you're sitting up straight, with your feet flat on the ground. If standing, double-check your posture.

STEP ONE: Breathe in through your nose for four counts.

STEP TWO: Hold this breath for four counts.

STEP THREE: Exhale through your mouth for four counts.

STEP FOUR: Hold this breath for four counts.

Rinse and repeat.

As you go through these steps, focus your attention on the sensation of your breath moving in and out of your body. You should notice that it starts to slow, along with the slowing of your heart rate.

It's tough to will yourself to relax, so try combining the square breathing method with a focus on relaxing your body. Start with your toes, and imagine they are perfectly relaxed. Once your toes are calm, visualize this feeling slowly traveling up your ankles, to your calves, through your knees and thighs, and upwards to the top of your head. When you can, give yourself a deep, long stretch with your arms above your head and then down to the floor. How does your breathing feel now? Do you notice a greater opening in your chest?

This practice helps us become more centered and calm and can also help us become more aware of any tension or discomfort we may be holding in our bodies. As we move on, our breathing becomes the foundation of all other mindfulness techniques.

Grounding Practices

One technique that can help you become more mindful is to practice grounding yourself in the present moment. This can involve using your senses to connect with your surroundings, such as noticing the feel of the ground beneath your feet, the sound of birds chirping in the distance, or the taste of your morning coffee. By focusing on these sensory experiences, you can anchor yourself in the present moment and become more aware of your thoughts and feelings without getting lost.

Focus on **one** thing that can bring you to the present. Touch the wall and focus on the texture. What color are the flowers outside? What color is the sky? How's the weather? How does the sun feel on your skin? Be present and accept what you're going through, but slow your thoughts down by zeroing in on something specific while you maintain deep breathing.

Other Mindfulness Practices

There are many different approaches to mindfulness, including meditation, yoga, and breathing exercises as we've discussed. Each of these practices can be helpful in cultivating a greater sense of calm and peace, but give each one a try to see which works best for you.

Meditation, for example, involves focusing your attention on a specific object, such as your breath, a mantra, or a visualization. The intention behind meditation is similar to that of deep breathing or grounding; we are trying to quiet the mind and become more present in the moment. Regular meditation practice can also help you become more self-aware and to cultivate a greater sense of compassion and acceptance toward yourself and others.

Yoga is another mindfulness practice with a wide range of benefits. This exercise involves moving your body in a series of postures, or asanas, while fo sing on your breath. This can help you become more aware of your body and how you breathe, and can also help you cultivate greater flexibility, strength, and balance. There are infinite types of yoga - from low impact and flowy to more intense and physical. Make sure you speak with your doctor before starting any new type of fitness routine, and we recommend starting with a low-impact yoga practice, such as restorative or vinyasa yoga.

By engaging in these practices regularly, you can begin to develop a greater sense of clarity and perspective, which can help you navigate life's challenges with greater ease and grace. This frees up space in your mind to focus on self-love.

Meditating with Positive Results

One way to use meditation to promote self-love and positivity is to incorporate positive affirmations into your practice. This can involve repeating a positive affirmation to yourself, such as "I am worthy and deserving of love and happiness," while focusing your attention on your breath or a specific object.

Another way to use meditation to promote self-love is to focus on a specific part of your body that you may struggle to accept or appreciate. For example, if you struggle with your body image, you could focus on your body during your meditation practice and repeat a positive affirmation to yourself, such as "I accept and appreciate my body exactly as it is."

Meditation is not one-size-fits-all. The key to successful meditation is to find a practice and environment that helps you settle your mind and reflect. For some, this is a more traditional meditation practice of sitting in a calm, quiet space and repeating their mantras and affirmations. For others, this is sitting on the beach or in their favorite outdoor spot, listening to music that calms their souls. Whatever this practice is for you is exactly right.

Journaling for Self-Love

Journaling can be a powerful tool for cultivating self-love and acceptance. By writing down your thoughts and feelings, you can gain greater clarity and insight into your patterns and tendencies and work to shift them in a more positive direction. We've recommended journaling throughout this book for several different things - from writing and reflecting on past experiences to making notes about triggers and toxic relationships. There is power in writing down our experiences, thoughts, or even quick notes about fleeting feelings. When these experiences, thoughts, and feelings have subsided, our journal entries allow us to reflect with a calm, collected mind. This is a vital piece of self-love: We can't work on what we don't understand or remember.

Practicing Gratitude

Focusing on gratitude can be a powerful way to increase feelings of self-love and happiness. By focusing on the things that you are grateful for in your life, you can cultivate a greater sense of appreciation and joy, which can help you navigate life's challenges with ease and grace.

One of the easiest ways to remind ourselves of what we're grateful for is to simply write them down each day - yet another example of how helpful keeping a journal can be. Keeping a log of the things that made us happy and grateful each day will help us become more aware of the blessings in our lives that we might otherwise take for granted.

Daily reflections are another way to practice gratitude and might work best for those who don't particularly enjoy journaling (or don't do it consistently). Take a few moments each day to reflect on the things you are grateful for. This can involve simply taking a few deep breaths and focusing your attention on the things that you appreciate in your life, such as your health, your relationships, or your career. In these moments of realizing how grateful you are for someone, **tell them!** Gratitude is a contagious practice, and sharing our warm and positive feelings of joy and appreciation is a fun and easy way to put positive energy out into the world.

Positive Affirmations

Positive affirmations are not strictly for meditation. They can be used independently of this practice and are a powerful way to remind ourselves of our power and our self-worth (see Chapter 9 for more on self-esteem and self-worth). By repeating positive affirmations to yourself, you can begin to shift your internal dialogue in a more positive direction, which can increase feelings of self-love and acceptance.

Some examples of positive affirmations include "I am worthy and deserving of love and happiness," "I am enough exactly as I am," and "I choose to love and accept myself unconditionally." By repeating these affirmations to yourself on a regular basis, you can begin to rewire your brain to focus on the positive aspects of yourself and your life.

Embracing Self-Love through Mindfulness Practices

Practicing mindfulness can be a powerful way to cultivate self-love and acceptance. By becoming more aware of our thoughts and feelings and by using mindful practices such as meditation, yoga, and breathing exercises, we can begin to shift our internal dialogue in a more positive direction, which can increase feelings of self-love and happiness.

By incorporating techniques such as grounding practice, journaling, practicing gratitude, and using positive affirmations, we can deepen our mindfulness practice and cultivate a greater sense of self-love. So if you're ready to start prioritizing your relationship with yourself, I encourage you to incorporate these mindfulness practices into your daily routine. Your mind, body, and soul will thank you for it.

CONCLUSION

After exploring the 11 strategies for developing self-love in women, it is clear that the journey to self-love requires a deep understanding of oneself, a willingness to let go of perfectionism, and the ability to control one's negative thoughts and emotions. It also involves recognizing that toxic relationships and lack of boundaries can hinder self-love. Practicing self-care, managing stress, and building self-esteem and self-worth are crucial components of this journey.

Growing as an empowered woman and engaging in daily self-love practices are essential for maintaining self-love over time. By following these strategies, women can cultivate a deep and lasting sense of self-love, which can positively impact all aspects of their lives.

Above all, these practices and the development of self-love provide us each the opportunity to grow in empathy, in compassion, and in the ability to connect with others and share our experiences and knowledge. I hope you've learned something from reading this book, and I hope you feel encouraged and excited to share it with those you love!

When we come together in a community, we have the opportunity to share experiences, offer advice, and provide emotional support. This is especially important when it comes to self-love, as it can be challenging to develop and maintain on one's own. By creating a community of women who are committed to similar goals, individuals can build a network of support that encourages growth and development.

In my experience, living among strong, like-minded women and in positive communities helps remind us of our value and worth, helps us build each other up, and allows us to cultivate deep and lasting senses of self-worth. Loving each other and loving ourselves are one and in the same, and I hope you find and build a community that helps you continue on through this journey.

And don't forget, I've created a journal template for you to use on the next page. You can upload it to your computer or print copies for yourself. My hope is this makes your daily journey easier, and that it helps you on your journey to self-love!

All the best in love and harmony,

Carolyn

Resources

Chapter One
https://emilysquotes.com/to-remember-who-you-are-you-need-to-forget-what-they-told-you-to-be/
https://www.unwomen.org/en/digital-library/multimedia/2020/2/infographic-visualizing-the-data-womens-representation
https://transitionandthrivewithmaria.com/why-is-self-care-so-hard-for-women/
https://winningandworthy.com/4-simple-reasons-why-women-struggle-with-self-love/
https://blog.opencounseling.com/how-can-understanding-your-past-help-you-in-the-present/
https://www.evergreenjournals.com/blogs/guides/why-reflecting-on-your-past-will-become-reflected-in-your-future
https://psychcentral.com/blog/ready-set-journal-64-journaling-prompts-for-self-discovery#the-journal-prompts
https://thegoalchaser.com/perfectionism-quotes/

Chapter Two
https://www.salon.com/2021/04/30/what-women-know-about-the-science-of-perfectionism/
https://time.com/70558/its-not-you-its-science-how-perfectionism-holds-women-back/
https://www.theguardian.com/commentisfree/2016/oct/14/perfect-girls-five-women-stories-mental-health
https://reachingself.com/why-we-should-embrace-being-wrong-practice-doubt-skill/
https://tinybuddha.com/blog/let-go-past-mistakes-6-steps-forgiving/
https://psychcentral.com/lib/tips-to-forgive-yourself#why-self-forgiveness-is-hard
https://positivepsychology.com/self-acceptance/

https://www.happiness.com/magazine/personal-growth/self-acceptance/

Chapter Three
https://www.verywellmind.com/negative-bias-4589618
https://andieandal.com/gender-stereotypes-part-negative-biases/
https://www.psychologytoday.com/intl/basics/toxic-positivity
https://www.mindbodygreen.com/articles/ways-to-stop-overthinking
https://bebrainfit.com/automatic-negative-thoughts/
https://www.nhs.uk/every-mind-matters/mental-wellbeing-tips/self-help-cbt-techniques/reframing-unhelpful-thoughts/
https://www.healthline.com/health/the-science-of-habit#3

Chapter Four
https://www.novabenefits.com/blog/the-art-of-self-love-and-emotional-intelligence
https://www.flyfivesel.org/article/the-purpose-of-emotions/
https://www.orionphilosophy.com/stoic-blog/viktor-frankl-greatest-quotes
https://hbr.org/2016/11/3-ways-to-better-understand-your-emotions
https://www.betterup.com/blog/emotional-regulation-skills
https://www.webmd.com/balance/features/how-to-be-more-empathetic

Chapter Five
https://www.womenshealthmag.com/relationships/a35799092/toxic-people/

https://www.healthline.com/health/toxic-relationship#signs-of-toxicity
https://www.wikihow.com/Be-an-Assertive-Woman
https://juliekantor.com/8-tips-building-assertive-communication-skills-woman/
https://www.forbes.com/health/mind/what-is-gaslighting/
https://www.delawarepsychologicalservices.com/post/7-ways-to-remove-toxic-people-from-your-life

Chapter Six
https://www.bonobology.com/types-boundaries-relationships/
https://www.gotquestions.org/spiritual-boundaries.html
https://believeandcreate.com/setting-boundaries-healthy-self-love/
https://psychcentral.com/blog/how-to-figure-out-your-boundaries#6
https://everydayfeminism.com/2016/09/figure-out-your-boundaries/
https://headway.ginger.io/3-kind-simple-effective-ways-to-communicate-your-boundaries-46dad0989e79
https://psychcentral.com/blog/imperfect/2016/07/how-to-deal-with-people-who-repeatedly-violate-your-boundaries#First,-lets-consider-a-few-of-the-variables:
https://limetreecounseling.com/healthy-boundary-counseling/
https://www.powerofpositivity.com/5-ways-to-respond-to-people-who-violate-your-boundaries/
https://www.reallifecounselling.com/2022/06/what-to-do-when-someone-crosses-your-boundaries-again/

Chapter Seven

https://www.tulipandsage.com/stop-feeling-guilty-about-self-care/
https://minimalism.co/articles/nutrition-and-self-care
https://www.mayoclinic.org/prebiotics-probiotics-and-your-health/art-20390058
https://eu.womensbest.com/blogs/health/5-self-care-tips-to-transform-your-fitness
https://13stripesfitness.com/blog-cat/strongtips-for-making-exercise-part-of-your-self-care-routine-strong/
https://www.amherst.edu/campuslife/health-safety-wellness/counseling/wellness/self-care-and-stress-reduction/sleep-well
https://www.ncbi.nlm.nih.gov/pmc/articles/PMC7320888/
https://balancethroughsimplicity.com/decluttering-as-self-care/
https://www.abtmarkets.com/abt-blog/practicing-financial-self-care

Chapter Eight

https://my.clevelandclinic.org/health/articles/5545-women-and-stress
https://www.sciencedirect.com/science/article/pii/S0002934322001371
https://www.webmd.com/balance/guide/tips-to-control-stress
https://my.clevelandclinic.org/health/articles/11874-stress
https://www.nhs.uk/mental-health/self-help/guides-tools-and-activities/tips-to-reduce-stress/
https://www.healthline.com/nutrition/16-ways-relieve-stress-anxiety#The-bottom-line
https://www.allied-services.org/news/2020/june/the-vagus-nerve-your-secret-weapon-in-fighting-s/

https://wellbeing.lifeworks.com/ca/blog/the-importance-of-self-love-positivity-self-esteem-and-resilience/
https://www.happify.com/hd/grow-resilient-by-building-self-worth/

Chapter Nine

https://positivepsychology.com/self-esteem/
https://au.reachout.com/articles/10-tips-for-improving-your-self-esteem
https://www.skillsyouneed.com/ps/self-esteem.html
https://www.nhs.uk/mental-health/self-help/tips-and-support/raise-low-self-esteem/
https://thehalcyonmovement.org/comparing-yourself-to-others-why-its-risky/
https://www.inc.com/lolly-daskal/19-simple-ways-to-boost-your-self-esteem-quickly.html
https://positivepsychology.com/self-worth/
https://indianschoolofimage.com/2021/09/15/6-ways-to-know-your-value-and-self-worth/

Chapter Ten

https://www.futurelearn.com/info/blog/general/develop-growth-mindset
https://www.berkeleywellbeing.com/self-growth.html
https://www.shinesheets.com/personal-growth-ideas-for-women-who-feel-lost-in-life/
https://www.sonyastattmann.com/personal-growth-for-women/
https://mindbodysynergies.com/goal-setting/
https://pennydevalk.com/5-successful-goal-setting-tips-for-female-leaders

Chapter Eleven

https://www.headspace.com/mindfulness/self-love

https://psychcentral.com/health/everyday-mindfulness#mindfulness-while-waiting
https://www.happify.com/hd/7-ways-to-be-mindful-in-your-everyday-life/
https://www.headspace.com/mindfulness/self-love
https://yogainternational.com/article/view/guided-meditation-for-self-love/
https://womensmeditationnetwork.com/self-love-meditation-shower-yourself-with-love/
https://mindfulzen.co/self-love-meditation/#3-5-minute-self-love-meditation-script
https://musingsfromthemoon.com/blogs/blog/25-self-love-journal-promptshttps://www.ta
https://www.betterup.com/blog/gratitude-definition-how-to-practice
https://positivepsychology.com/daily-affirmations/
https://www.mindtools.com/air49f4/using-affirmations

Additional Resources
https://www.webmd.com/balance/stress-management/stress-management
https://www.mayoclinichealthsystem.org/hometown-health/speaking-of-health/5-tips-to-manage-stress
https://www.travis.af.mil/News/Commentaries/Display/Article/2149823/manage-stress-before-it-manages-you/
https://www.iese.edu/insight/articles/how-manage-stress/
https://www.cdc.gov/violenceprevention/about/coping with-stresstips.html
https://health.gov/myhealthfinder/health-conditions/heart-health/manage-stress
https://www.heart.org/en/healthy-living/healthy-lifestyle/stress-management/3-tips-to-manage-stress
https://www.betterup.com/blog/stress-management-techniques

https://www.cci.health.wa.gov.au/Resources/Looking-After-Yourself/Self-Esteem
https://fetzer.org/sites/default/files/images/stories/pdf/selfmeasures/Self_Measures_for_Self-Esteem_ROSENBERG_SELF-ESTEEM.pdf
https://positivepsychology.com/self-worth/
https://www.choosingtherapy.com/self-worth-vs-self-esteem/
https://medium.com/@karwickca/do-panic-attacks-kill-because-i-might-be-dying-57b955897bf6

Made in United States
Orlando, FL
27 November 2024